PROHIBITION

Social Movement and Controversial Amendment

By Joan Stoltman

Portions of this book originally appeared in
Prohibition by John M. Dunn.

LUCENT
PRESS

Published in 2019 by
Lucent Press, an Imprint of Greenhaven Publishing, LLC
353 3rd Avenue
Suite 255
New York, NY 10010

Designer: Deanna Paternostro
Editor: Jessica Moore

Cataloging-in-Publication Data

Names: Stoltman, Joan.
Title: Prohibition: social movement and controversial amendment / Joan Stoltman.
Description: New York : Lucent Press, 2019. | Series: American history | Includes index.
Identifiers: ISBN 9781534564145 (pbk.) | ISBN 9781534564121 (library bound) | ISBN 9781534564138 (ebook)
Subjects: LCSH: Prohibition--United States--Juvenile literature. | United States--History--20th century--Juvenile literature.
Classification: LCC HV5089.S76 2019 | DDC 363.4'10973--dc23

Printed in the United States of America

CPSIA compliance information: Batch #BS18KL: For further information contact Greenhaven Publishing LLC, New York, New York at 1-844-317-7404.

Please visit our website, www.greenhavenpublishing.com. For a free color catalog of all our high-quality books, call toll free 1-844-317-7404 or fax 1-844-317-7405.

Contents

Foreword   4

Setting the Scene: A Timeline   6

Introduction:
Americans and Alcohol   8

Chapter One:
Early Attempts at Prohibition   15

Chapter Two:
The Movement Toward Prohibition Begins   21

Chapter Three:
The Rebirth of the Prohibition Movement   33

Chapter Four:
The 18th Amendment   49

Chapter Five:
Lawlessness Ravages the Country   57

Chapter Six:
The Push for Repeal   80

Epilogue:
The Effects of Prohibition   89

Notes   93

For More Information   97

Index   99

Picture Credits   103

About the Author   104

Foreword

The United States is a relatively young country. It has existed as its own nation for more than 200 years, but compared to nations such as China that have existed since ancient times, it is still in its infancy. However, the United States has grown and accomplished much since its birth in 1776. What started as a loose confederation of former British colonies has grown into a major world power whose influence is felt around the globe.

How did the United States manage to develop into a global superpower in such a short time? The answer lies in a close study of its unique history. The story of America is unlike any other—filled with colorful characters, a variety of exciting settings, and events too incredible to be anything other than true.

Too often, the experience of history is lost among the basic facts: names, dates, places, laws, treaties, and battles. These fill countless textbooks, but they are rarely compelling on their own. Far more interesting are the stories that surround those basic facts. It is in discovering those stories

that students are able to see history as a subject filled with life—and a subject that says as much about the present as it does about the past.

The titles in this series allow readers to immerse themselves in the action at pivotal historical moments. They also encourage readers to discuss complex issues in American history—many of which still affect Americans today. These include racism, states' rights, civil liberties, and many other topics that are in the news today but have their roots in the earliest days of America. As such, readers are encouraged to think critically about history and current events.

Each title is filled with excellent tools for research and analysis. Fully cited quotations from historical figures, letters, speeches, and documents provide students with firsthand accounts of major events. Primary sources bring authority to the text, as well. Sidebars highlight these quotes and primary sources, as well as interesting figures and events. Annotated bibliographies allow students to locate and evaluate sources for further information on the subject.

A deep understanding of America's past is necessary to understand its present and its future. Sometimes you have to look back in order to see how to best move forward, and that is certainly true when writing the next chapter in the American story.

1600s
The triangular trade establishes an exchange of slaves from Africa for rum made in the colonies.

1874
The Woman's Christian Temperance Union (WCTU) is founded.

1791
The Whiskey Rebellion begins and lasts for four years.

1600s	1784	1791	1826	1874	1917

1826
The American Temperance Society is founded in Boston, Massachusetts.

1917
The U.S. Senate and House of Representatives approve the 18th Amendment on December 18.

1784
Dr. Benjamin Rush publishes *An Inquiry into the Effect of Spirituous Liquors on the Human Body and Mind, and Their Influence upon the Happiness of Society*, igniting the first major temperance movement.

A Timeline

1920
The 18th Amendment and the Volstead Act take effect.

1933
The 21st Amendment quickly passes through Congress and the states, ending Prohibition.

| 1919 | 1920 | 1926 | 1929 | 1933 |

1919
Nebraska's ratification of the 18th Amendment makes Prohibition a national law.

1926
The U.S. Senate subcommittee holds hearings in April on the effects of Prohibition.

1929
Gangster violence hits a bloody high with the St. Valentine's Day Massacre on February 14 in Chicago, Illinois.

Introduction

AMERICANS AND ALCOHOL

When Europeans arrived in the New World, provisions aboard Christopher Columbus's ships the *Niña* and *Pinta* included rations of red wine for each passenger. A little more than a century later, ships transporting English settlers to North America carried wooden barrels of beer on board. Even the strictly religious Puritans, religious pilgrims from England, transported so-called "hot waters" on the *Mayflower* to quench their thirst. In fact, they transported more beer than water to America. Water could not be relied on during the journey or in the New World because of deadly waterborne diseases.

In the colonies, breakfasts commonly began with a small drink of cider, rum, whiskey, or brandy. Colonists believed these drinks, sometimes called "bitters," provided energy for the coming day. They also drank to stay warm in winter and because they thought it restored vital fluids when they sweated in summer. As the Colonial Williamsburg Foundation published,

> Many started the day with a pick-me-up and ended it with a put-me-down. Between those liquid milestones, they also might enjoy a midmorning whistle wetter, a luncheon libation, an afternoon accompaniment, and a supper snort. If circumstances allowed, they could ease the day with several rounds at a tavern.[1]

Laborers took drinking breaks throughout the workday with an alcoholic beverage supplied by employers to keep their workers strong and happy. Church bells sometimes rang to announce such daytime liquor recesses. Drinking alcohol was a popular pastime in colonial America. It may have even saved lives because water was often contaminated, especially in large cities with high populations such as Boston, Massachusetts. Diseases such as typhoid (a disease that consists of stomach pain, loss of appetite, high fever, and headache), dysentery (a disease that consists of severe diarrhea), and leptospirosis (a bacterial disease that includes high fevers, headaches, rash, chills, vomiting, diarrhea, and more) spread throughout the water easily. This means a meal that may typically have had a glass of water with it would have an alcoholic beverage instead because the water was not safe to drink.

Social Drinking in the Colonies

Drinking also occurred at local taverns as colonists gathered to socialize. Historians believe that many important political moments that led up to the American Revolution happened in taverns over drinks. Wherever colonists gathered, even colonial children, alcohol flowed. According to journalist Eric Burns,

in some colonial schools, the books were put aside for a few minutes each morning and afternoon so that the children, who might not have gotten enough liquor upon awakening, could be given a few more tastes to revive their flagging attention.[2]

Many Americans drank while they visited with each other, shopped, served in court, and attended events such as barn raisings and quilting parties. Some drank alcohol to the point of drunkenness at funerals. Burns noted that during the colonial period,

men and women from all stations of life were laid to rest with portions of rum in their caskets, a little something to ease the passage from one world to the next. Even paupers were so equipped.[3]

Among the most favored early imports was rum, a hard liquor manufactured in the West Indies that was distilled from molasses. In the 1650s, colonists began distilling rum for themselves, providing many jobs that were steady and respectable. By 1770, the product was an essential part of the economy because international demand for rum was at a fever pitch.

Colonial companies dispatched sailing ships loaded with rum to Europe. Then, European goods were exchanged for African slaves who were then transported to the West Indies to be sold for molasses. That molasses was shipped back to the colonies to make rum. The slave trade became known as triangular trade because of the route from the colonies to Europe to Africa and back to the colonies that was taken again and again.

Taverns often played a central role in the political and social lives of colonists.

In the Army

Colonial troops during the American Revolution received a daily ration of 8 ounces (236.6 ml) of rum to ward off the winter chill, supplement meager food rations, lift spirits, instill courage, and, it was believed, keep the men fit and healthy. This policy would continue for decades. General Marvin Kilman, a commander in the Continental Army, once observed that "much of George Washington's continuing good cheer and famed fortitude during the long years of the war … may have come from the bottle."[4]

This bottle of rum is from 1772 and belonged to a man from colonial Massachusetts.

The New Country Drinks

In 1776, the Declaration of Independence was signed while overflowing amounts of alcohol were consumed by its signers, including "54 bottles of Madeira, 60 of Claret, 22 of port, 8 hard cider, 12 beers, 7 bowls of alcoholic punch and 8 bottles of Whiskey."[5] Many Americans drank heartily to celebrate their hard-won independence, although drinking to drown wartime sorrows was not uncommon. For many former soldiers, drinking together in a saloon became a way of continuing a brotherhood forged in battle. "To be drunk was to be free," historian W. J. Rorabaugh wrote. "The freedom that intoxication symbolized led Americans to feel that imbibing lustily was a fitting way for independent men to celebrate their country's independence."[6]

After the war, the new nation began its great experiment with self-government. By the time Americans went to war against Great Britain in 1812, technological changes, steady immigration, and new economic and social conditions all contributed to an increase in public alcohol consumption. By the 19th century, the nation was awash with alcohol. By 1810, the average American adult drank 7 gallons (26.5 L) of alcohol a

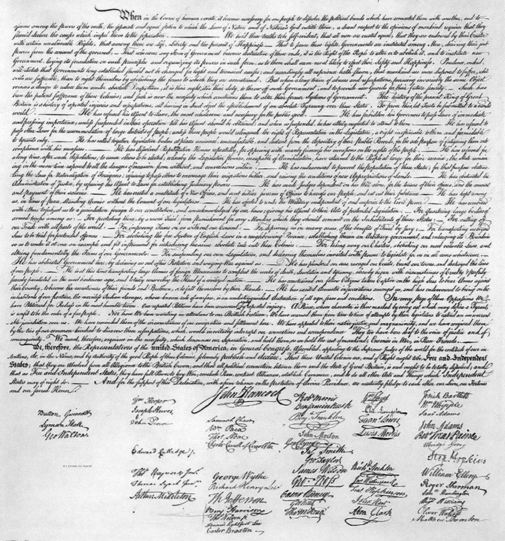

During the signing of the Declaration of Independence, shown here, the men who signed it were drinking a number of alcoholic beverages, including whiskey and beer.

year. A decade later, that number rose to 10 gallons (37.9 L) per person. Although men were the heaviest drinkers, they were by no means alone in consuming alcohol. Calculations in 1826 estimated that women and children drank 1.3 gallons (5 L) of alcohol annually, although most of the consumption was still by men, who drank nearly 20 gallons (75.7 L) a year. This sentiment from a Savannah, Georgia, resident in 1829 described the era's drinking habit: "If I take a settler after my coffee, a cooler at nine, a bracer at ten, a whetter at eleven, and two or three stiffeners during the forenoon, who has a right to complain?"[7] Horace Greeley, an editor and political figure who grew up in the 1820s, also described that in his childhood, "there was scarcely a casual gathering of two or three neighbors for an evening's social chat, without strong drink."[8]

Chapter One

EARLY ATTEMPTS AT PROHIBITION

Despite the general acceptance of alcohol in colonial America, there were notable exceptions. The strict Puritans of the Massachusetts Bay Colony publicly whipped drunkards or forced them to wear a scarlet-colored "D" around their neck to publicly humiliate them, sometimes for as long as a year. In the 1670s, Puritan leader Increase Mather explained, "Drink is itself a good creature of God, and to be received with thankfulness, but the abuse of drink is from Satan, The wine is from God, but the Drunkard is from the Devil."[9] However, the most extreme example of colonial-era prohibition can be found in the story of Georgia.

America's First Attempt at Prohibition

The founder and first governor of Georgia, Englishman James Oglethorpe, wanted the new colony to be alcohol-free. He allowed the settlers to use small amounts of beer and molasses to sweeten livestock feed, but to his great disappointment, some used the molasses to make rum. Infuriated, Oglethorpe promoted the creation of the London Trustees Act of 1735, which declared that "no Rum, Brandies, Spirits or Strong Waters"[10] could enter the colony. It also called for sellers to be punished as lawbreakers and hard liquor confiscated and destroyed.

The intention was to spread morality among the colonists, but corruption quickly surfaced. Colonial officials accepted bribes to look the other way, smugglers snuck hard liquor in from nearby colonies, and some settlers even set up their own illegal distilleries in remote areas. America's first attempt at prohibition had failed, and the laws were reversed by 1742. The reaction of Georgia's first colonists to prohibition laws provided a preview of how future attempts at alcohol restrictions through law would go down in America. Without fail, some Americans reacted by smuggling, illegally distilling, and bribing, but some

This is a rendering of the plan for Savannah, the capital of the Georgia colony. James Oglethorpe's vision for the colony was to give debtors who were in prison in England a new lease on life through moral guidance, but some people hesitated at his rules enforcing prohibition and banning slavery.

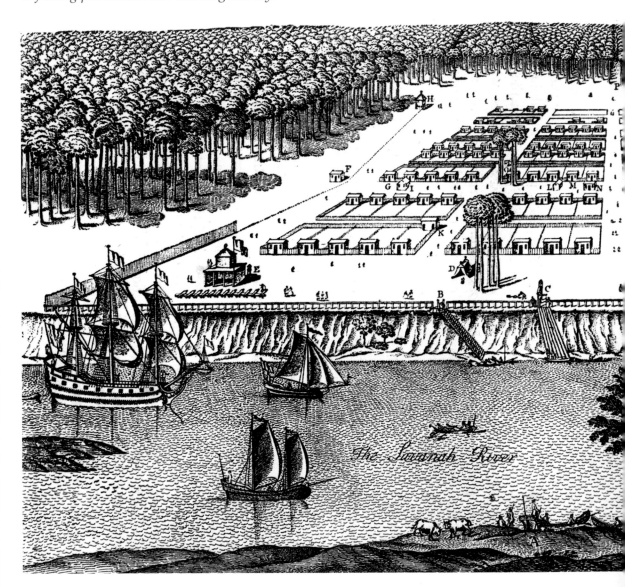

attempts at prohibition would also turn violent.

The Rising Concern

Georgia's early attempt at prohibition sparked a debate on drinking alcohol in the colonies. Concerns mounted over reports of spousal and child abuse and neglect, fights, injuries, idleness, and other social ills. Quakers, Methodists, and other religious groups began to speak out against drunkenness. They argued that excessive drinking was morally depraved, ungodly, and destructive to human life. Many even went as far as to call drunkenness a sin. These concerned voices, however, soon lost their position as colonists geared up to fight for their independence from England. The country would soon be engulfed in war.

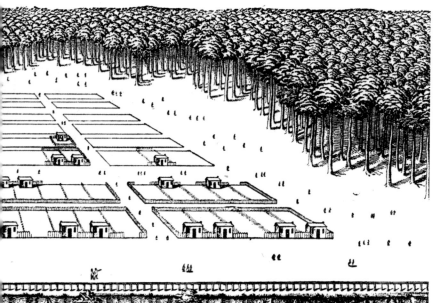

The Alcohol Problem Returns

Following the end of the American Revolution, many farmers in western Pennsylvania found it cheaper and more profitable to convert corn and rye into alcohol and ship it to markets in the East rather than pay to transport the bulky grain to eastern distilleries to process. There was good money to be made: a bushel of corn yielded about 25 cents, but

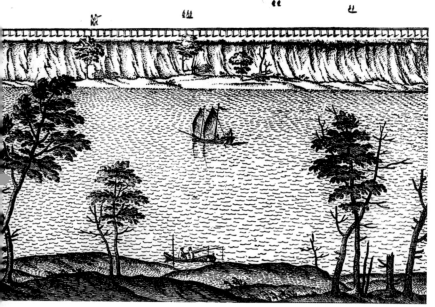

that same bushel made into whiskey earned four to five times as much.

The distribution of alcohol was seen as a unique opportunity by the nation's first secretary of the treasury, Alexander Hamilton. He proposed a national tax on whiskey, arguing that it would raise badly needed revenues to pay off war debts and show citizens the power of the new federal government. The tax, he noted, should also work to encourage Americans to reduce their drinking. Hamilton—who limited himself to three glasses of wine a day—was seen as a model of moderation, evidence as to how common drinking had become. As he pointed out in a 1790 report to Congress:

> the consumption of ardent spirits particularly, no doubt very much on account of their cheapness, is carried to an extreme, which is truly to be regretted, as well in regard to the health and the morals, as to the economy of the community. Should the increase of duties [taxes] tend to a decrease of the consumption of those articles, the effect would be, in every respect desirable.[11]

Congress began imposing the tax in 1791 throughout the country, quickly infuriating the financially strapped Pennsylvania farmers. They refused to pay the new tax; after all, a war had just been waged over the freedom from taxation without representation. Their insubordination was significant, as many of the men were veterans of the American Revolution. They also tarred and feathered tax collectors and burned down the distilleries of neighbors who paid the tax.

Alarmed at the growing Whiskey Rebellion, Hamilton persuaded President George Washington to send more than 12,000 militia troops into western Pennsylvania in 1794 to stop the uprising. The farmers dispersed and reluctantly paid the tax. The new tax enriched federal government funds, but it did little to suppress American thirst for alcohol as Hamilton had hoped.

Increasingly, Americans began discussing the effects of alcohol on individuals and society once again. One of those Americans was Dr. Benjamin Rush, who was a ferocious enemy of alcohol. Rush argued against the practice of giving alcohol to soldiers, which was something Washington and others had done during the American Revolution.

Dr. Benjamin Rush

Dispensing alcohol to men at war made no sense to Dr. Benjamin Rush. In 1778, he published his disagreement with wartime rum rationing, arguing that alcohol was actually the cause of many diseases that plagued soldiers. This publication marked one of the earliest instances when alcohol use was attacked for non-religious reasons. After the war, Rush gathered what he had learned on the battlefield and in 1785 published a more comprehensive and influential work—*An Inquiry into the Effect of Spirituous Liquors on the Human Body and Mind, and Their*

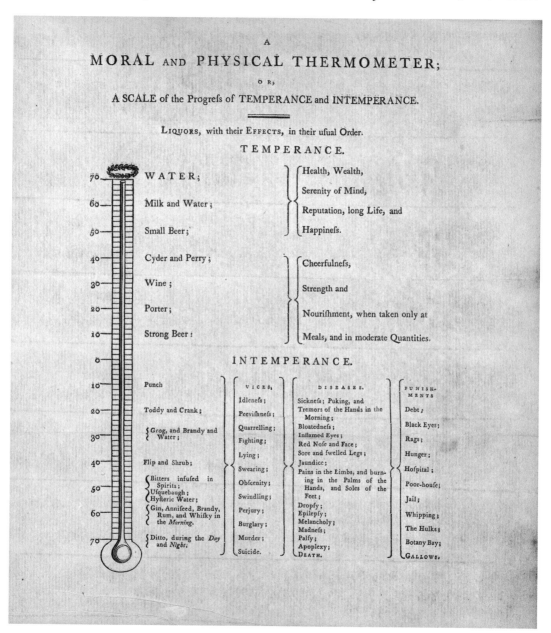

Dr. Benjamin Rush's "moral thermometer" suggested that drinking water leads to health and wealth and drinking liquor day and night led to the gallows, or hanging.

Rush Questions Rum Rations

Dr. Benjamin Rush expressed misgivings about soldiers receiving rations of alcohol in his pamphlet, "Directions for Preserving the Health of Soldiers":

The common apology for the use of rum in our army is that it is necessary to guard against the effects of heat and cold. But I maintain that in no case whatever does rum abate the effects of either upon the constitution. On the contrary, I believe it always increases them. The temporary elevation of spirits in summer, and the temporary generation of warmth in winter, produced by rum, always leave the body languid and more liable to be affected with heat and cold afterwards ... The use of rum, by gradually wearing away the powers of the system, lays the foundation of fevers, fluxes, jaundices, and the most of diseases which occur in military hospitals. It is a vulgar error to suppose that the fatigue arising from violent exercise or hard labour is relieved by the use of spirituous liquors.[1]

1. Quoted in Richard Eddy, *Universalism in America: A History*, vol. 1. Boston, MA: Universalist Publishing House, 1884, p. 317.

Influence upon the Happiness of Society. The 40-page booklet included a "moral thermometer,"[12] a chart that showed his imaginative view of the various vices, diseases, and punishments drinkers could expect in their lifetime, depending on what they drank and how often.

Chapter Two

THE MOVEMENT TOWARD PROHIBITION BEGINS

As surgeon general of the Continental Army and a professor of chemistry and medicine, Benjamin Rush's opinions on liquor held powerful influence. His booklet sold tens of thousands of copies by 1815 and was reprinted for three decades. It was also quoted in almanacs, newspapers, and periodicals. His captivated readers would soon launch the first national temperance movement in America. Many ministers stopped serving liquor to their congregations. Methodist and Presbyterian churches called upon their members to give up all alcoholic beverages. Many factory owners cracked down on employees drinking at work.

Toward the end of his life, Rush had great hopes for the movement, saying that by 1915, a drunk person will "be as infamous in society as a liar or a thief, and the use of spirits as uncommon in families as a drink made of a solution of arsenic or a decoction [a liquid preparation involving boiling a plant] of hemlock."[13]

The First Group

Billy James Clark, a country doctor in upstate New York, sounded an alarm after reading Rush's booklet, declaring, "we shall all become a community of drunkards in this town unless something is done to arrest the progress of intemperance [excessive drinking]."[14] Clark invited a small group of like-minded men to a meeting at a local schoolhouse on April 30, 1808. They formed the Union Temperance Society of Moreau and Northumberland and pledged to stop drinking hard liquor for a year. News of Clark's group spread, and many similar temperance groups soon appeared in New York, New England, and the Midwest.

The largest of these was the American Temperance Society, an organization that vowed to shutter the nation's 4,000 distilleries. Founded in 1826 in Boston, Massachusetts, the organization soon boasted 8,000 local chapters and more than 1 million members. Members publicly pledged to moderate their drinking, although some vowed to abstain altogether. The letters "TA" were written next to the names of these "total abstainers" on membership rosters, giving rise to the "teetotaler," a term still used today to describe a person who does not drink alcohol.

The early temperance movement in the South was never as strong as it was in the North. Many white southerners were hesitant to support a movement whose northern members were likely to also support the abolition of slavery—a practice that supported their economic foundation.

Approaches to Temperance

Within a few years, approximately 5,000 anti-drinking societies had formed in the country with a wide range of temperance goals. Some wanted to close all distilleries and drinking establishments. Others sympathized with heavy drinkers and attempted to redeem them. Still others concentrated on convincing moderate drinkers to shun liquor or to drink only beer and wine. More radical activists insisted that the only liquid worth drinking was water.

Few temperance groups sought to push for laws to moderate or ban alcohol at this point. Instead, they focused on persuasion and education with a goal to change human behavior. Supporters believed individuals should make up their own minds about drinking, often pointing to Oglethorpe's failure in Georgia as a reminder that laws regarding human behavior would not succeed.

Morality Resurfaces

As the temperance movement grew, many felt that the medical approach of Rush was not as convincing as an appeal to the emotions. However, the growing religious and moral tone of temperance did not hold a singular position. Many religious leaders labeled alcoholics and drunks as lapsed Christians whose souls were doomed, while others argued that drunkenness was proof of humanity's fall from the grace of God.

Temperance reformers now quoted Reverend Lyman Beecher, a Litchfield, Connecticut, preacher who published a collection of anti-drinking sermons in 1825. His book, *Six Sermons on the Nature, Occasions, Signs, Evils and Remedy of Intemperance*, argued that alcohol damaged the physical, mental, and spiritual health of the individual:

Whoever, to sustain the body, or invigorate the mind, or cheer the heart, applies habitually the stimulus of ardent spirits, does violence to the laws of his nature, puts the whole system into disorder ...

I ask liberty Mr President to present a Resolution in respect to the traffic in ardent spirit. I feel prepared to advocate the extension of the fundamental principle of your society - viz. total abstinence - to this traffic - and that too on the principles of the Bible. If any should feel surprised that the Resolution which I have in my hand holds forth such decided language on this subject I can only say that to me it seems clear that the future historian of temperance will be more astonished that it was necessary in the year 1831 to enter into an argument to prove that the principles of the Bible did not admit of the traffic in ardent spirit except as a medicine - or a convenient solvent for the Chemist's Laboratory - Or rather I apprehend that this subject will hereafter be viewed very much as every conscientious man now regards the slave trade. But if John Newton could continue for some time after his conversion to aid in that murderous traffic without feeling the reproof of conscience I can easily believe that many Christians equally sincere & conscientious with him may now be employed in a traffic no less murderous in its effects. I would therefore affectionately reason out of the Scriptures with every one in the

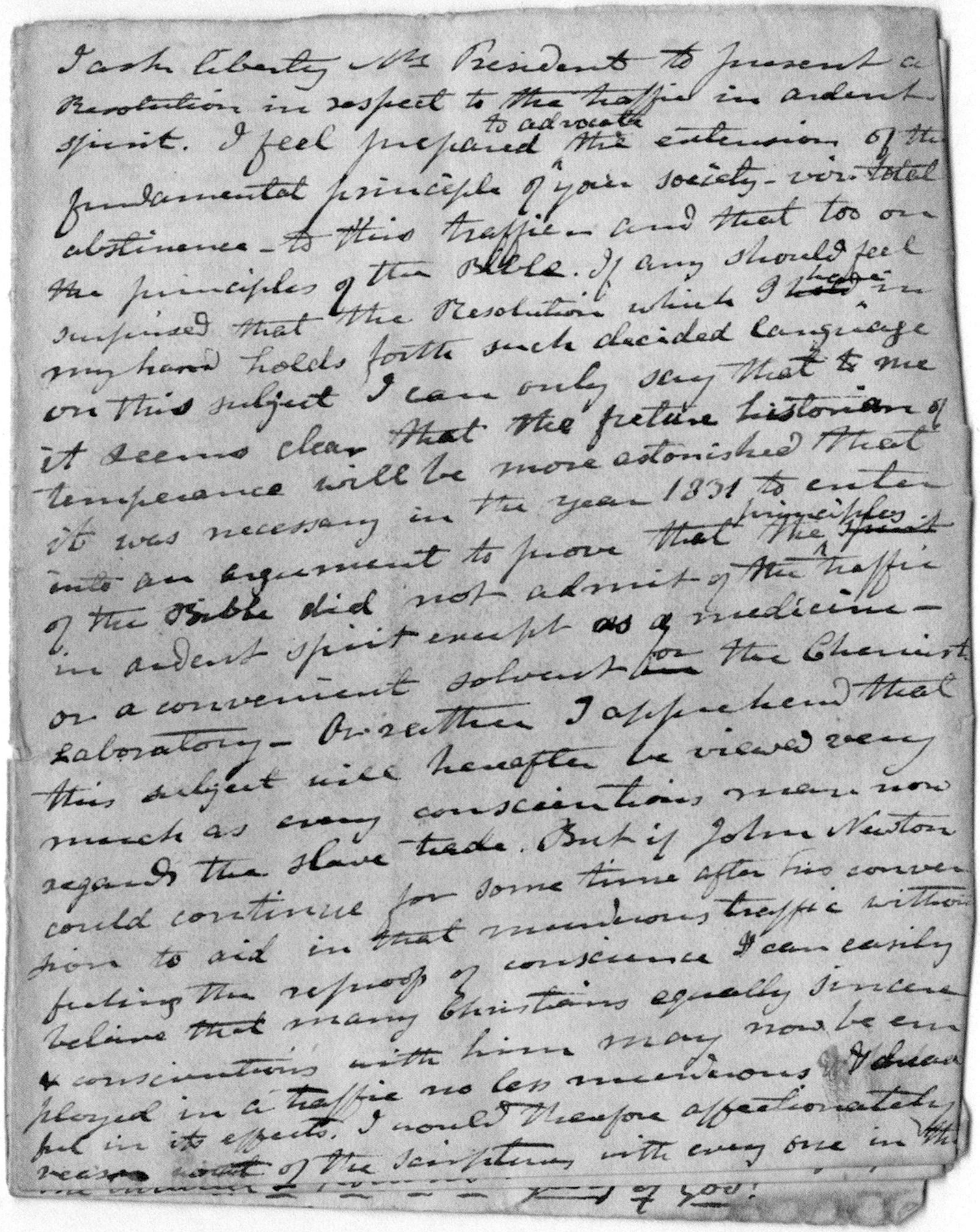

In his 1837 speech to the American Temperance Society, Edward Hitchcock said that selling liquor was inconsistent with both Christianity and the cause of temperance, despite the seller not participating in drinking. Notes from the speech are shown here.

Reverend Lyman Beecher's collection of pro-temperance essays had widespread influence on the growing anti-alcohol movement.

Spontaneous Ignition

Temperance speakers enthralled audiences across the nation with tales of heavy drinkers so steeped in alcohol that they suddenly burst into flames. It did not matter that it was not true. Minister W. R. G. Mellen of the Unitarian Church in Dover, New Hampshire, told of one such encounter with spontaneous combustion in March 1882:

A young man, about twenty-five years of age … had been a habitual drinker for many years. I saw him about nine o'clock in the evening on which it happened. He was … as usual, not drunk, but full of liquor. About eleven the same evening I was called to see him. I found him literally roasted from the crown of his head to the soles of his feet. He was found in a blacksmith's shop just across the way from where he had been. The owner all of the sudden discovered an extensive light in his shop as though the whole building was in one general flame… and on flinging open the door discovered a man standing erect in the midst of a widely extended silver-colored blaze, bearing, as he described it, exactly the appearance of the wick of a burning candle in the midst of its own flame …

There was no fire in the shop, neither was there any possibility of fire having been communicated to him from any external source—It was purely a case of spontaneous ignition.[1]

1. Quoted in "The Temperance Movement," Dover Public Library, accessed January 16, 2018. www.dover.nh.gov/government/city-operations/library/history/the-temperance-movement.html.

It is the moral ruin which it works in the soul, that gives it the denomination of giant-wickedness.[15]

Beecher hit a nerve across America. Clergy everywhere quoted his words from their pulpits. They were reprinted for more than a decade and eventually became the core text for the next phase of the temperance movement. Soon, public anti-alcohol speakers held crowds across the nation spellbound with lurid tales that focused on the perils and evils of drinking. Brochures, articles, novels, songs, and plays that portrayed lurid accounts of drunkards who abused and neglected their loved ones also cropped up during this wave of anti-alcohol fervor.

Reverend Justin Edwards of Boston, Massachusetts, published a "Temperance Manual" that spread like wildfire in the 1830s. In it, he rejected the centuries-old idea that liquor was a pleasure given from God, arguing that such a notion was as different from God's life-affirming creation as "poison is from food, sickness from health, drunkenness from sobriety."[16] He also declared that drinking was harmful and pushed for total abstinence. Scorn was also heaped upon saloons and other businesses that sold alcohol. Reverend Mark Matthews of Seattle, Washington, remarked, "The saloon is the most fiendish [and] corrupt … institution that ever crawled out of the slime of the eternal pit."[17]

Disagreement Among the Movement

Reformers across the country realized the need to band together and work with a single purpose, but they could not agree on common goals or tactics. Those favoring temperance still favored using moral persuasion, biblical scripture, and public shame to get others to join their cause. Others wanted to pressure lawmakers to ban hard liquor, if not all alcoholic drinks. Reformers also debated whether to ignore drunkards and instead focus on the task of convincing moderate drinkers to give up drinking—or should the producers and sellers of alcohol be their primary targets? These debates caused disunity. The temperance movement was in danger of losing its momentum.

Converts

The movement was revived thanks to the work of six heavy drinkers from Baltimore, Maryland. On the night of April 2, 1840, two of the men attended a temperance lecture, expecting to be entertained. Instead, they were captivated and converted to total abstinence, and they convinced their drinking partners to join in their abstinence. Along with other reformed drinkers, the men formed the Washingtonian Temperance Society of Baltimore.

Their meetings, where former heavy drinkers stood before their peers to relate personal stories of how alcohol had ruined their lives, proved to be powerful events. Hundreds of curious people soon flocked to the meetings and listened to the group's message of experience and inspiration instead of religious condemnation. Chapters formed across the nation, attracting hundreds of thousands of new members. A women's version of the movement, called Martha Washington Societies, was formed in New York with a special focus on the abuse and hardship that women and children suffered at the hands of alcoholic men.

Children's Temperance Organizations

A temperance organization for children, called the Cold Water Army, also

Medals and coins such as the medal shown here were frequently given to members of temperance organizations.

emerged. It was founded by Thomas P. Hunt, a Presbyterian minister, who believed that temperance energies were better spent teaching children to avoid the dangers of alcohol rather than trying to help hard-to-reform adult drinkers. In Cold Water Army chapters across the country, children pledged to drink cold water instead of alcohol and marched through busy city streets, waving banners and singing temperance songs.

The Movement Reaches Some Consensus

By the 1850s, the Washingtonian Temperance Society had disbanded because of a lack of organization and unity. However, other popular groups took its place, such as the Sons of Temperance, which had 6,000 units and 200,000 members; Templars of Honor and Temperance; the Independent Order of Good Templars; and other similar organizations.

Convinced that neither persuasion

A Cold Water Army Pledge

The Cold Water Army, an organization for children with an anti-alcohol mission, created a pledge for members that stated that the girls and boys would:

*Freely renounce the
treacherous joys*

*Of brandy, whiskey, rum,
and gin,*

*The Serpent's lure to death
and sin ...*

*Wine, beer, and cider
we detest,*

*And thus we'll make our
parents blest,*

*So here we pledge
perpetual hate*

To all that can intoxicate.[1]

1. Quoted in George Batchelor, *Personal Reminiscences*. Boston, MA: Press of Geo. H. Ellis Co., 1916, p. 5.

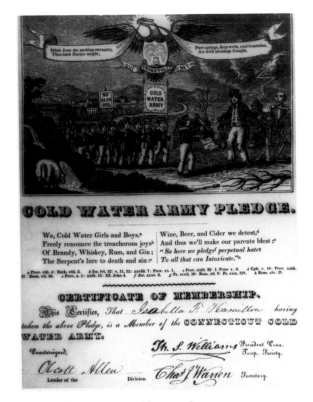

Shown here is a certificate of membership for the Connecticut branch of the Cold Water Army.

nor an appeal to emotion and religion had done much to sway most American drinkers, many reformers now clamored for laws to make the changes in their society that they felt were so necessary. A growing number of activists now wanted the very thing many early temperance supporters had hoped to avoid: laws that criminalized drinking.

Changes to laws, however, seemed possible, particularly state laws. An 1847 U.S. Supreme Court decision resolved that the Constitution did not forbid state governments from regulating or banning the sale of liquor. This judicial decision came as a shock to the liquor dealers who had filed the lawsuit in the first place with the hope that it would result in a legal decision banning prohibition at the state level.

Disagreements once again flared up among the ranks of the anti-alcohol forces over what to do. Some wanted to work for the passage of laws that allowed local governments to restrict or ban the issuing of new liquor licenses to businesses. Others argued that legislation was needed that forbid the drinking, manufacturing, or sale of only hard liquor or all intoxicating beverages.

Maine Takes a Stand

Reformers went to work lobbying local and state lawmakers to pass anti-alcohol laws using legal precedents in place from earlier attempts at making alcohol illegal. Maine had already passed several laws in 1821 and 1826 that punished various liquor infractions, but this was not enough regulation for Neal Dow, a Quaker from Portland, Maine. Dow was determined to make prohibition, not temperance, the law of his native state.

As Portland's fire chief, Dow had once ordered his crew to leave a liquor store burning. The story bolstered his reputation as a stern crusader for prohibition, even though he denied that it had happened. After forming the Maine Temperance Union in 1838, he left his job and dedicated his life to the cause, traveling thousands of miles in a door-to-door effort to urge 40,000 citizens to sign his anti-alcohol petition and vote for prohibitionist candidates.

Thanks to Dow, Maine outlawed alcohol across the state in 1846. However, Maine's anti-prohibition governor vetoed a companion bill in 1849 that required state officials to enforce prohibition, leaving the job to local authorities. By 1850, prohibitionists controlled Maine's state legislature, and by the next year, they had passed a new statewide prohibition law—one designed by Dow himself—that banned the sale of alcoholic beverages and imposed a tough enforcement policy that included raids, fines, and imprisonment. Maine had officially gone "dry."

The Maine law caused controversy across the nation. Supporters agreed with Reverend Beecher's assessment of Maine: "God's work every step of the way."[18] Critics were appalled by Dow's ongoing liquor raids and called supporters of the law "Maine-iacs" and Dow the "Napoleon of Temperance." In 1852, Vermont, Massachusetts, Rhode Island, Oregon, and Minnesota passed their own "Maine" laws. Connecticut took action in 1854.

Strict prohibitionist Neal Dow led Maine to become the first dry state in 1851.

By 1855 Indiana, Delaware, Nebraska Territory, Michigan, Pennsylvania, New York, and New Hampshire had passed their own prohibition laws, and several other states had only been narrowly defeated in their efforts. A tide of state prohibition was sweeping the nation.

Enforcing State Prohibition

Enforcing the new prohibition laws proved much harder than passing them. Many people quickly found loopholes in the new laws. Unethical doctors began prescribing alcohol as medicine for patients willing to pay them a fee, a practice that would continue through the 1930s. Many sidestepped laws by purchasing liquor through the postal system from another state.

There was also violent backlash. A rum riot broke out in Portland, Maine, on June 2, 1855. An angry mob, many of whom were Irish immigrants upset that prohibition seemed directed at their alcohol-drinking culture, stormed City Hall. Dow, now the mayor of Portland, called the local militia and personally gave the order to fire at the mob. When the shooting stopped, one lay dead, and many were wounded.

Attempts to criminalize alcohol faltered similarly in many states. Most of the new anti-alcohol laws would be repealed in the wake of violence, legal challenges, or revocation by state governments. The failure of the state prohibition laws left many Americans wondering if banning alcohol was a worthy goal. Many now agreed with Abraham Lincoln, who in 1840, told his fellow representatives in the Illinois state legislature that "prohibition goes beyond the bounds of reason in that it attempts to control a man's appetite by legislation and makes crimes out of things that are not crimes."[19]

The End of the First Wave of Prohibition

All questions of temperance and prohibition were soon overshadowed by a national crisis: the American Civil War. Not only did it preoccupy people and politics for four years, but it caused a major law to be passed that gave anti-prohibitionists an edge in the political battle. Congress passed the Internal Revenue Act in 1862 to finance the Union war effort. Among other things, it imposed a fee on the production of liquor, ale, and beer. Temperance advocates were too quick to assume this would reduce alcohol consumption. Rather, Burns wrote, "what the taxes did, for the first time, was make the liquor industry an important part of the American economy."[20]

Many assumed the tax would expire when the war ended, but it continued for decades afterward. Government officials had become accustomed to the revenues it provided the federal government, and some even hoped for increased liquor sales to provide even more funding.

Proponents of temperance had a lost cause on their hands when the war ended in 1865.

New drinking problems, however, soon emerged as many disillusioned soldiers returned home and turned to alcohol to escape the trauma of war. America also became more urbanized, as displaced farmers and rural residents moved to cities to find work. Low pay and squalid living and working conditions drove many people to saloons to drink away their woes.

Chapter Three

THE REBIRTH OF THE PROHIBITION MOVEMENT

In the late 19th century, American society still operated under tightly held beliefs about women's roles in the home and their required obedience and silence on serious matters. Soon, however, women would rise up with a powerful campaign against saloons. It all began in 1873 with Diocletian Lewis, a self-proclaimed doctor, writer, and public speaker who had enthralled audiences for 20 years with a boyhood story about his mother and other local church women who had banded together in song and prayer to close the saloons in his small town.

The Women's Crusades

Eliza J. Thompson of Hillsboro, Ohio, a town with a population of 5,000, believed she had received a spiritual calling to protest alcohol when she heard Lewis's story. Gathering more than 100 like-minded women, Thompson's group marched through town, descending upon the local drinking establishments with songs, prayers, and Bible verses. Shamed and embarrassed, the owners of all 21 liquor-selling businesses, including 13 saloons, closed.

"Mother Thompson and her Visitation Band" inspired women across Ohio to form temperance groups of their own. Sometimes groups even demanded that saloonkeepers close their doors or risk their supply of alcohol being destroyed. Lewis continued his public speeches, voicing support for the growing women's crusade. Convinced they were carrying out God's will, tens of thousands of women crusaded across the Midwest and in West Virginia, New York, Oregon, and California.

An Account of Raiding a Tavern

In the following excerpt from a 1927 article in the *Milwaukee Journal*, writer Mary A. Hartwell recalled a time more than 70 years earlier when she and other women of Baraboo, Wisconsin, launched raids on local taverns. Hartwell wrote,

> As half the women approached the front of the hotel, Pete appeared at a window with a shotgun in his hand. "If any woman dares try to enter this place, I will shoot to kill," he threatened.

> And, at the same time, the other half of the women were at the back door, pouring Pete's liquor upon the ground so that it ran in rivulets down the street. Oh, that was great!

> There were some folks there, of course, that looked right sad as they saw the liquor going to waste, but most of 'em were in sympathy with the women.[1]

1. "A Bottle Smashing Crusader of Wisconsin," Wisconsin Historical Society, accessed January 18, 2018. www.wisconsinhistory.org/turningpoints/search.asp?id=1291.

Reaction to Women's Crusades

The women's crusades often provoked ridicule, anger, and violence from saloon owners and customers. Threats, jeers, obscenities, and insults rained down upon the women as they protested. They were attacked, spit on, and soaked with dirty water and beer. Some angry saloon proprietors set dogs loose on demonstrators. The 70-year-old president of the Temperance League of Bucyrus, Ohio, was even dragged through the streets. According to newspapers of the day, the women crusaders were also

> drenched with paint; accosted with water from pumps and hoses; pelted with rotten eggs, stones, old boots, and even bricks; threatened by mobs so large and violent that police protection was inadequate; and forced by husbands to leave the streets. One spouse even publicly horsewhipped his wife for her participation.[21]

Police often broke up these demonstrations and jailed the women only to see them back on the streets after their release, once again protesting against alcohol.

An End and a Beginning

The women's crusade began to run out of steam by the summer of 1874. Many of the saloons they had closed reopened as the marches and demonstrations faded, but the momentum for a national prohibition movement was officially beginning again. The women's crusade had succeeded in publicizing temperance issues, inspiring the revival of temperance groups, and encouraging women to organize and work together for a single purpose. Many women began speaking out against the serious social problem of drunkenness. Millions of women now had a newfound feeling of purpose and accomplishment. They were also experiencing, at long last, the power of political activism.

Many veterans of the women's crusade decided that their next step was

This illustration from the 1800s depicts a women's crusade liquor raid. Their protests temporarily closed thousands of bars and saloons across much of America and inspired a movement.

to form a more disciplined, national organization. In November 1874, they met in Cleveland, Ohio, to consolidate various state organizations and form the Woman's Christian Temperance Union (WCTU).

Frances Willard Leads the Way

At the helm of the WCTU was Frances Willard, a former educator, daughter of pioneers, and an experienced temperance activist. An accomplished writer, public speaker, and advocate of women's rights, she was attracted to the temperance movement because she admired the way women had taken over a crusade left unfinished by men. She was also an ardent opponent of saloons, convinced that they contributed to the dominance men held in society by excluding women from public life.

However, the same struggles of purpose and organization that had plagued other temperance groups before them plagued the WCTU. A faction of wealthy, conservative women wanted to focus solely on temperance. Willard's faction argued that the organization should widen its scope to include an array of social and economic problems plaguing American society, such as poverty, disease, and squalid living conditions. These issues, she argued, all affected one other.

Willard's faction soon took control of the WCTU and became a powerful advocate for many progressive causes under her able leadership. In addition

to its battle against alcohol abuse, the WCTU encouraged women from all walks of life to learn more about nutritional cooking, gardening, health, and exercise. It supported the women's suffrage (voting) movement, civil service reform, Native American rights, and labor unions. However, the WCTU never lost sight of its main mission: to abolish liquor through laws at the state and local levels.

Temperance Lawmaking Efforts

Many WCTU members called for a constitutional amendment to prohibit liquor nationwide. To accomplish this goal, Willard launched a national campaign to build popular support. The WCTU distributed books, pamphlets, newspapers, magazines, and other documents calling for a ban on alcohol, and they organized public speaking engagements about the evils of "demon rum." WCTU volunteers circulated petitions, formed pressure groups, and lobbied lawmakers.

Convinced that drinking alcohol was deeply etched into American society, WCTU leadership decided to take its message directly to America's youth. In 1886, the group created an anti-drinking educational campaign in state public schools. During this period, Congress mandated WCTU's educational programs for schools under federal control in Washington, D.C., and in U.S. territories.

In addition to promoting education,

The WCTU produced cards such as the one shown here to encourage others to support a ban on alcohol.

the WCTU became politically active by supporting the Prohibition Party, a national political party founded in 1869. WCTU leaders felt the only way to close loopholes in state prohibition laws was to bring their own political party to power and bring about change through legislation. All of these efforts were successfully operating in tandem when Willard suddenly died at age 59. She was mourned and praised by many Americans, and she became the first woman to be represented in Statuary Hall in the U.S. Capitol in Washington, D.C.

Her 1898 death permanently weakened the organization she had grown to national prominence. Willard was personally associated with the identity of the organization and was the driving force behind so many of its efforts. The WCTU ceased to be the same powerful social, moral, and political force in America.

Campaigning Against Saloons

America's saloons became the target of prohibition efforts in the 1890s. Saloons were common features of everyday life, with 1 licensed saloon for every 300 people and tens of thousands of unlicensed, illegal saloons beyond that. Some establishments were richly decorated and served wealthy patrons. Many saloons, however, were unsanitary and rundown buildings frequented by heavy drinkers, gamblers, and sex workers. "The most notable thing about the saloon was its stink," wrote historian Donald Barr Chidsey. "It was a fusty, musty odor, damp and clammy, an odor compounded of sawdust, tobacco juice, malt, metal polish, and whiskey."[22]

In saloons, many intoxicated men ruined their health, squandered their savings, and neglected their families. Americans watched the daily dramas of neighborhood saloons with disgust and alarm. Local governments occasionally took action against saloons, but they remained popular gathering places for many Americans, and thus they became targets of prohibitionists.

Baseball Player Turned Prohibitionist

Billy Sunday was one of America's most beloved and outspoken foes of saloons. Once a frequenter of saloons, he gave up alcohol after listening to the songs and testimonials at the Pacific Garden Rescue Mission in Chicago, Illinois, in 1887. Within a few years, the baseball player had become a traveling evangelical preacher and zealous campaigner against saloons and alcohol. With a mix of showmanship and humor, Sunday spread his views on alcohol abuse, singling out the saloon as a great evil. He preached that the saloon was a thief that "robs you of manhood and leaves you in rags and takes away your friends, and it robs your family. It impoverishes your children and it brings insanity and suicide."[23]

Free from scandal, wholesome, and sincere, Sunday had hundreds of

Born into poverty in Iowa, Billy Sunday played professional baseball before becoming a leader in the movement against saloons.

In this photograph, a large crowd of people can be seen waiting for Billy Sunday's arrival in New York City.

thousands of followers and made a lot of money. His magnetism attracted many people to the national prohibition movement.

The Woman Who Took a Hatchet to Saloons

While Billy Sunday was adored by millions, the public was less sure what to make of the most notorious enemy of saloons—a controversial woman willing to use violence in the name of God. Carry Nation was an aggressive reformer who had suffered a drunk grandfather during childhood and a drunk first husband. She left her husband within the first year of their marriage, and he died six months after she left.

Remarried and new to Medicine Lodge, Kansas, Nation helped to found a chapter of the Kansas WCTU in 1889. Saloons in Kansas openly sold alcohol in defiance of the state's prohibition laws. At first, she tried the WCTU way: singing and praying. When that did not work, she confronted customers at the saloon doors, calling them names and begging them to give up drinking. In 1900, she said she

Carry Nation took a more aggressive approach to temperance than other individuals and destroyed saloons and liquor bottles. Many people disliked her, as can be seen on this hatchet-shaped sign, which was carved with "All Nations Welcome But Carrie."

received a revelation from God with the solution. Nation later recalled the message: "'Take something in your hands, and throw at these places in Kiowa and smash them.' I was very much relieved and overjoyed and was determined to be 'obedient to the heavenly vision.'"[24]

Nation barged into the saloons in the small town of Kiowa, Kansas, wielding bricks, rocks, scrap metal, and pieces of wood at liquor bottles and bar room property. She also wielded a hatchet, which became her trademark. She described herself as "a bulldog running along at the feet of Jesus, barking at what he doesn't like."[25] When Kiowa police threatened to jail her for destruction of private property, she retorted that she had destroyed illegal alcoholic beverages and therefore broke no law. She walked away free.

Next, Nation and other like-minded women attacked saloons in Wichita, Kansas, destroying bottles and kegs of liquor, plate-glass windows, paintings, and other property. "I came to the Governor's home town … to destroy the finest saloon in it," she said, "hoping thus to attract public attention to the flagrant violation of a Kansas law under the very eye of the chief executive of the state."[26] Authorities arrested her more than 30 times during her spree of attacks that lasted through March 1901.

Nation often engaged in other questionable acts. She celebrated the assassination of President William McKinley in 1901, because, she said, he drank alcohol and got what he deserved. She even published an open letter in the *Topeka Daily Capital* calling children to violence:

I send you greetings and ask you to help me destroy that which is on the streets and protected by the police and the city officials to destroy you, my darlings. I want every one of you little ones to grab up a rock and smash the glass doors and windows of these [places]. You will do your duty and enroll your name on the pages of undying fame, and place yourself on the side of God and humanity.[27]

The publicity eventually cost her membership in the WCTU, and despite her good intentions, she became a figure of public ridicule.

The "Male Carry Nation"

Often called the "Male Carry Nation," William Johnson was another aggressive prohibitionist. He was known for damaging illegal saloons and smashing alcohol bottles while carrying weapons, and he also arrested lawbreakers.

In 1881, Johnson's lifelong opposition to alcohol led him to work with anti-alcohol forces in Nebraska who hoped to make prohibition part of the state constitution. Once, he even posed as a brewery owner to gain access to alcohol industry information, which he then published for the nation to read. In 1906, while working as a

When William "Pussyfoot" Johnson returned east after serving as a federal agent in the Oklahoma Territory, he took over a publishing plant tasked with printing propaganda for the Anti-Saloon League.

lobbyist for prohibition in Washington, D.C., President Theodore Roosevelt sent him to the Oklahoma Territory to lead an effort against the illegal liquor trade that was devastating Native Americans.

When Johnson and his men raided illegal liquor dealers throughout the territory, his quiet, cat-like manner of sneaking up on his prey earned him the nickname "Pussyfoot." He was known to wear a cowboy hat and long coat and carry a rifle when he and his men performed raids, which sometimes resulted in fistfights or shoot-outs. Upon learning that a saloonkeeper had sworn to kill him, an infuriated Johnson disguised himself, rode into town on a horse, sauntered into the bar, and arrested him. By the time Pussyfoot Johnson left the Native American territory in 1911, he had overseen about 6,000 arrests.

The Anti-Saloon League

Founded in 1893, the Anti-Saloon League (ASL) wanted to close down Ohio's saloons. The league also had a bigger prize in mind: a national ban on alcohol. Much of the organization's strength lay in how it was structured. Its membership was a vast confederation of churches of many denominations. The churches were both vehicles for carrying out temperance work and sources of revenue for the movement.

Wayne B. Wheeler, an attorney from Ohio, took charge of the organization in 1901 and soon proved himself to be a shrewd leader. He became a powerful political figure in both Ohio and national politics, and he possessed so much influence that he could rally enough voters to oust any elected officials who opposed the league.

By 1919, Wheeler had led the organization to national prominence through years of strategy. First, the ASL helped prohibition candidates win city and county positions. These local political bases were then used to launch bigger campaigns for state and federal positions. The league favored no political party; it backed any candidate who voiced promises to support prohibition laws. If all candidates for a position were pro-alcohol—or "wets," as people were calling them—the league would find its own "dry" candidate to run for the job.

A National Victory is Won

By 1905, state-level prohibition was only in effect in Kansas, Maine, and North Dakota. The ASL and its allies organized an effort that succeeded in bringing Tennessee, North Carolina, Georgia, Oklahoma, and Mississippi into the fold within four years. These gains were notably agricultural states in the South and the Midwest, as prohibition was most successful with rural, religious, and conservative people.

Millions of Americans continued to drink heavily in the dry states. Trainloads filled with crates of bottled liquor

Wayne B. Wheeler witnessed a drunken person scare his sisters and mother. In addition, a drunken farmhand had accidentally wounded Wheeler with a pitchfork when Wheeler was young. These bitter memories spurred him to fight for national prohibition. Many other temperance leaders had similar stories.

rattled into dry states from neighboring wet states every day, making a mockery of the new dry laws. The ASL responded by persuading U.S. senator William S. Kenyon of Iowa and North Carolina representative Edwin Y. Webb to draft legislation that enabled state governments, instead of the federal government, to regulate train shipments of liquor across state borders. Congress approved the bill in 1913, but President William Howard Taft vetoed, or rejected, it, claiming it violated the Constitution by curbing the federal government's right to regulate commerce. Congress, however, overrode Taft's veto with the necessary two-thirds majority vote. The U.S. Supreme Court later ruled that the law was constitutional.

This powerful show of national-level support demonstrated that prohibitionists were no longer merely a regional political force in farming states. Some political observers were so impressed with the league's demonstration of power that they predicted it was only a matter of time before prohibition at the national level became a reality.

The 16th Amendment

A major blow to alcohol interests came in 1913 when the passage of the 16th Amendment authorized Congress to levy taxes on personal incomes, thus making it harder for opponents of prohibition to argue that Americans needed alcohol taxes to raise revenue for the government. In that same year, the 17th Amendment was passed, and

for the first time ever, the American people voted for their representatives in the U.S. Senate. Prohibitionists could now exponentially increase opportunities to influence laws by electing prohibitionist senators into office.

In 1914, several prohibitionist representatives took seats in Congress, but the ASL was not yet sure it had enough seats to get a two-thirds majority to pass a constitutional amendment. Prohibitionist legislators decided to find out how many seats they still needed by introducing a resolution on December 22 to call for a debate on the issue. The House voted, revealing 197 legislators in favor of prohibition and 190 against it.

At War with Germany

While prohibitionist representatives were gaining momentum in Congress, World War I had begun in Europe. The United States remained neutral at first, but soon public sentiment tilted increasingly against Germany. When German submarines sunk the *Lusitania* in 1915, 128 American travelers had died. In early 1917, Germany tried unsuccessfully to convince Mexico to join them in a war against the United States. The United States formally declared war on Germany on April 6, 1917.

Prohibitionists acted quickly to use the wartime sentiments against Germany for their own purposes. They made beer an unpatriotic drink and rained criticism down on the beer industry. Some extremists even proclaimed that German-American brewers were traitors and spies.

The ASL pushed prohibitionist congressmen to pass legislation that ensured all grains and other foodstuffs were used to feed American soldiers, sailors, and allies and not used to make liquor. It was wrong, they said, to divert grain to the liquor industry to make alcoholic drinks instead of using the grain to make bread.

Next, anti-prohibition lawmakers pushed for a bill that included a ban on using grains to make liquor. President Woodrow Wilson wanted to make sure sufficient grain supplies were delivered to U.S. military personnel, but he also opposed a law that lowered the federal taxes the alcohol industry would have to pay during a war. Seeking a compromise, he persuaded prohibitionist legislators to withdraw their controversial part of the food bill by promising that prohibition would be part of future legislation.

Feeling like Wilson had not acted quickly enough on that promise, leading prohibitionist congressmen voted to ban the use of grain for any beverage in 1917. The president believed that Congress would override any veto of his, so he signed the bill into law.

Chapter Four

THE 18TH AMENDMENT

The ASL first turned toward national prohibition as an official policy in 1913 at a national convention. In December 1913, 2,000 people from across the nation arrived in Washington, D.C., to attend a public demonstration organized by the ASL and the WCTU. They marched in the cold and snow along Pennsylvania Avenue from the White House to the Capitol building to demand that Congress pass the 18th Amendment to the Constitution to prohibit the sale and manufacture of alcohol in the entire country. Later that same day, sympathetic lawmakers presented bills to Congress written by the ASL, calling for the amendment process to begin.

Wayne B. Wheeler and the ASL, however, did not want to push Congress to vote on national prohibition until they had built strong political support for national prohibition among voters. A powerful political campaign soon got underway. Over the next year, the ASL printed and distributed letters and brochures to elected officials across the country.

They also circulated petitions and made speeches in support of prohibition candidates. Businesses with the most to lose if prohibition became law— namely the manufacturers, distributors, and retail sellers of liquor, beer, and wine—started to take part in the growing national debate. They struck back with angry words and political lobbying, but they were no match for the impassioned, well-organized, and well-financed temperance forces.

A Bill Becomes an Amendment

In 1917, prohibitionists forced Congress to discuss a proposed amendment to the Constitution regarding national

The Text of the 18th Amendment

The 18th amendment to the U.S. Constitution is sometimes misunderstood. It did not make drinking alcohol illegal; it simply banned the sale, creation, and transportation of alcohol. In full, the amendment reads:

Section 1.

After one year from the ratification of this article the manufacture, sale, or transportation of intoxicating liquors within, the importation thereof into, or the exportation thereof from the United States and all territory subject to the jurisdiction thereof for beverage purposes is hereby prohibited.

Section 2.

The Congress and the several states shall have concurrent power to enforce this article by appropriate legislation.

Section 3.

This article shall be inoperative unless it shall have been ratified as an amendment to the Constitution by the legislatures of the several states, as provided in the Constitution, within seven years from the date of the submission hereof to the states by the Congress.[1]

1. "18th Amendment," Cornell Law School, accessed January 19, 2018. www.law.cornell.edu/constitution/amendmentxviii.

prohibition. During heated arguments over the issue, anti-prohibitionists in the Senate made a big mistake. Confident that the amendment did not have support from at least 36 states needed to ratify it—even though by now 27 states had prohibition laws of some sort—they agreed to let the amendment go forward, provided that ratification by the states was completed within 6 years.

The Senate, followed by the House of Representatives, approved the 18th Amendment on December 18, 1917, with little fanfare. Prohibitionists were sure it would pass,

State	Date of Ratification	State	Date of Ratification
Mississippi	Jan. 8, 1918	Tennessee	Jan. 13, 1919
Virginia	Jan. 11, 1918	Washington	Jan. 13, 1919
Kentucky	Jan. 14, 1918	Alabama	Jan. 14, 1919
North Dakota	Jan. 25, 1918	Arkansas	Jan. 14, 1919
South Carolina	Jan. 28, 1918	Illinois	Jan. 14, 1919
Maryland	Feb. 13, 1918	Indiana	Jan. 14, 1919
Montana	Feb. 18, 1918	Kansas	Jan. 14, 1919
Texas	Mar. 14, 1918	North Carolina	Jan. 14, 1919
Delaware	Mar. 18, 1918	Colorado	Jan. 15, 1919
South Dakota	Mar. 20, 1918	Iowa	Jan. 15, 1919
Massachusetts	Apr. 2, 1918	New Hampshire	Jan. 15, 1919
Arizona	May 24, 1918	Oregon	Jan. 15, 1919
Georgia	June 26, 1918	Utah	Jan. 15, 1919
Louisiana	Aug. 8, 1918	Nebraska	Jan. 16, 1919
Florida	Nov. 27, 1918	Wyoming	Jan. 16, 1919
Michigan	Jan. 2, 1919	Minnesota	Jan. 17, 1919
Ohio	Jan. 7, 1919	Wisconsin	Jan. 17, 1919
Oklahoma	Jan. 7, 1919	New Mexico	Jan. 20, 1919
Idaho	Jan. 8, 1919	Nevada	Jan. 21, 1919
Maine	Jan. 8, 1919	New York	Jan. 29, 1919
West Virginia	Jan. 9, 1919	Vermont	Jan. 29, 1919
Missouri	Jan. 10, 1919	Pennsylvania	Feb. 25, 1919
California	Jan. 13, 1919	New Jersey	Mar. 10, 1922

Even though anti-prohibitionists did not think it would pass, the 18th amendment was quickly ratified across the United States, starting with Mississippi on January 8, 1918.

and anti-prohibitionists were sure it did not have enough support. The ratification time limit was extended to seven years. It was now down to the states to ratify the 18th Amendment into law.

As the states pondered the amendment proposal, congressional prohibitionists pushed through an emergency law—despite earlier assurances they would not do so—that imposed national wartime prohibition. Called the War-Time Prohibition Act, it did not go into effect until November 21, 1918, 10 days after World War I ended, but it would prove useful as they now argued that postwar America should also be alcohol-free.

One state after another quickly ratified the amendment. Contrary to what many anti-prohibition lawmakers had expected, there was huge support for prohibition in the country. Decades of propaganda and lobbying by the ASL and other temperance groups had convinced millions of Americans that the nation should abolish alcohol. By January 16, 1919, the Nebraska state legislature ratified the 18th Amendment, officially giving it approval from three-fourths of the states. With the ratification of this amendment, the prohibition movement had officially transformed into a formal Prohibition law and era.

A Flawed Amendment

Prohibitionists and anti-prohibitionists alike were astonished by how fast Prohibition had come upon them. They also realized that the newest amendment to the Constitution had flaws that had been overlooked as it was rushed through Congress.

The 18th Amendment, for example, banned the manufacture, sale, transport, import, and export of alcoholic beverages, but said nothing about buying and drinking liquor. Americans could still legally obtain alcohol—even if produced illegally—and store it in their homes. Nor did the new amendment explain how Prohibition would be enforced. Would enforcement be a federal responsibility or that of the states? Critics also pointed out that the Constitution guarantees all Americans the right to be secure in their homes. They warned that this right could be taken away if overzealous law enforcement

personnel felt compelled to raid private homes looking for alcohol.

Wayne B. Wheeler, working with House Judiciary Committee chairman Andrew J. Volstead of Minnesota and other lawmakers, tackled this issue by writing new legislation that sought a balance between enforcement of the law and protection of civil liberties. After undergoing many changes in both houses of Congress, the Volstead Act—as the lengthy and complicated measure was known—provided the legal basis for the enforcement of the 18th Amendment.

The Volstead Act Becomes Law

The Volstead Act faced a political hurdle in President Wilson, who had always been unenthusiastic about Prohibition. He vetoed the new law on October 27, stating, "In all matters having to do with the personal habits and customs of large numbers of our people, we must be certain the established processes of legal change are followed."[28]

Congress, however, quickly overrode his veto and made wartime Prohibition permanent. The Volstead Act would take effect at one minute after midnight on January 16, 1920.

Expectations of Prohibition

Millions of Americans cheered the passage of the Volstead Act. In their view, the long crusade to rid the country of a dangerous drug that caused death,

The Volstead Act

The 18th Amendment had many issues. The Volstead Act was written by the 66th Congress to close the loopholes of the constitutional amendment by specifying who would enforce Prohibition. Among other things, the act also defined "liquor" and added possession to the list of offenses:

The word "liquor" or the phrase "intoxicating liquor" shall be construed to include alcohol, brandy, whisky, rum, gin, beer, ale, porter, and wine, and in addition thereto any spirituous, vinous, malt, or fermented liquor, liquids, and compounds, whether medicated, proprietary, patented, or not, and by whatever name called, containing one-half of 1 [percent] or more of alcohol by volume which are fit for use for beverage purposes ...

No person shall on or after the date when the eighteenth amendment to the Constitution of the United States goes into effect, manufacture, sell, barter, transport, import, export, deliver, furnish or possess any intoxicating liquor except as authorized in this Act.[1]

1. Quoted in Linda De Roche, *The Jazz Age*. Santa Barbara, CA: ABC-CLIO, 2015, p 66.

---

dissolution, and despair had finally been achieved. Church bells pealed across the country to welcome the good news. Prohibitionists across America celebrated with ceremonies, public speeches, and noisy parades that featured actors dressed up as demons being run out of town.

Once the battle over Prohibition had been won, many people expected results that may seem farfetched today. Some dry towns believed so much that Prohibition would have transformative, almost miraculous, effects on society that they closed their jails. Economist Mark Thornton added to the list of expectations that "prohibitionists wanted and expected people to switch their spending from alcohol to dairy products, modern appliances, life insurance, savings, and education."[29] Historian Michael Lerner further clarified prohibitionist expectations following the passing of the 18th Amendment and the Volstead Act:

They expected sales of clothing and household goods to skyrocket. Real estate developers and landlords expected rents to rise as saloons closed and neighborhoods improved. Chewing gum, grape juice, and soft drink companies all expected growth. Theater producers expected new crowds as Americans looked for new ways to entertain themselves without alcohol.[30]

Billy Sunday announced this joyous news to his followers with a prediction of the societal changes to come: "The reign of tears is over. The slums will soon be a memory. We will turn our prisons into factories and our jails into storehouses and corncribs. Men will walk upright now, women will smile and children will laugh."[31]

Funerals for Alcohol

Not everyone, of course, was pleased. The country's liquor industry was shocked, and so were the millions of people who had fought the new ban. They faced the coming of Prohibition grim with anger and remorse. In the final hours before Prohibition became law, bars staged mock funerals for alcohol.

Many brought attention to James Oglethorpe's futile attempt to ban alcohol in Georgia as proof that the law would not be effective. They also argued that drinking was a private matter and could not be stamped out by govern-

ment decree. Enforcement would never work, they added, because the United States was too large to patrol. In addition, they pointed out, there were too many loopholes in the law, and resourceful Americans who wanted to obtain alcohol would always find ways to do so.

The day before Prohibition officially went into effect, a federal judge ruled that law enforcement officials could legally confiscate any liquor found outside a private dwelling, such as in businesses or vehicles. This news spurred many Americans to go on a shopping spree and buy as much alcohol as possible to store in their homes. Bars quickly sold their supplies as people hoarded wine, beer, and hard liquor. In private dwellings, many people believed, authorities could not intrude unless they obtained search warrants from judges, although this did not mean private stocks of liquor were safe. Many wealthy Americans found themselves robbed of their alcohol stashes during Prohibition; however, few predicted enforcement problems. They insisted that the majority of Americans were law-abiding citizens who had obeyed government authority during World War I's prohibition. Thus, they could be expected once again to do their patriotic duty and accept permanent Prohibition.

One such person who anticipated little trouble was John F. Kramer of Mansfield, Ohio, the first commissioner of the Prohibition Bureau—the

Many bar owners draped their establishments in black and staged mock funerals for alcohol. As their customers drank their last lawful drinks, liquor bottles were placed in a coffin.

federal government's newly created law enforcement agency. Kramer, in fact, suggested that enforcement costs would drop, as Americans became accustomed to Prohibition. However, Kramer was wrong.

The many officials at New York City's Office of the Medical Examiner predicted in December 1919 that Prohibition, "rather than making alcohol disappear, would instead create 'numerous harmful substitutes for whiskey.'"[32] However, even these scientists, who had begun to study the effects of alcohol on the body, could not truly fathom what was to come.

Chapter Five

LAWLESSNESS RAVAGES THE COUNTRY

People were determined to continue drinking. Thousands of makeshift distilleries, large and small, appeared seemingly overnight in forests and rural areas. Homegrown liquor producers set up stills in city apartments, basements, and the back rooms of stores and restaurants. Bathtubs in private homes served as preparation basins where amateur beverage makers mixed glycerin, water, and juniper oil with alcohol to produce so-called bathtub gin.

As the do-it-yourself movement grew, savvy book publishers sold an assortment of how-to books to help readers make alcohol at home. Public libraries also provided the books for their patrons. In addition, Americans could turn to popular magazine articles to get ideas on how to make alcoholic beverages. Lerner pointed out that "the law that was meant to stop Americans from drinking was instead turning many of them into experts on how to make it."[33]

Even the U.S. Department of Agriculture, which had provided information on home brewing before Prohibition, never stopped publishing brochures that explained how to create alcohol from a variety of foods, making these publications more popular than ever. The irony of the federal government providing this service during the Prohibition era was noted by author Eric Burns, who wrote, "The same folks who had passed the law forbidding liquor were now providing detailed instructions on how to break it."[34]

Enterprising merchants cashed in by marketing products that could be used to make alcohol. Various shops appeared everywhere that sold yeast, hops, and other

Americans were determined to drink alcohol. Some poured alcohol down hollow walking canes, capped them, and strapped canisters to one of their legs underneath a pair of trousers. Others hid flasks of whiskey in their garters or boots. Known as "bootlegging," this term was used to also describe trafficking in illegal alcohol.

Wine "Warnings"

Wine drinkers could purchase blocks or bricks of compressed grape mixtures that could be dropped into a pitcher and mixed with water to turn them into grape juice that could then be converted into wine. Many big city department stores hired saleswomen to explain to their customers the real intent of the product.

The following series of "warnings" from a New York salesgirl in a Fifth Avenue store is typical of their approach:

Do not place the liquid in this jug and put it away in the cupboard for twenty-one days, because then it would turn into wine.

Do not stop the bottle with this cork containing this patented red rubber siphon hose, because that is necessary only when fermentation is going on.

Do not put the end of the tube into a glass of water, because that helps to make the fermenting liquor tasty and potable [drinkable].

Do not shake the bottle once a day, because that makes the liquor work.[1]

1. Quoted in Robert Maddox, "The War Against Demon Rum," in *American History Volume 2: Reconstruction Through the Present*, ed. Robert Maddox. Guilford, CT: Dushkin, 1989, p. 103.

ingredients and brewing apparatuses needed for making beer at home. All this was legal, because the Volstead Act did not outlaw the sale or purchase of alcohol-making equipment. Even those individuals wanting to distill liquor had no problem buying special cookers and corn sugar mash, prepared for the home-whiskey maker. Primitive distillation was even possible with a teakettle and a towel.

The Business of Illegal Liquor

The federal government regulated the amount of alcohol a beverage could contain. Beer could contain 2 to 6 percent alcohol. Wine could contain 7 to 20 percent alcohol. Whiskey, a hard liquor, could contain 40 percent alcohol. However, during Prohibition, people who normally drank beer and wine now only had access to hard liquors. Thornton explained,

During Prohibition virtually all production, and therefore consumption, was of distilled spirits and fortified wines ...

Prohibition made it more difficult to supply weaker, bulkier products, such as beer, than stronger, compact products, such as whiskey, because the largest cost of selling an illegal product is avoiding detection.[35]

With only access to hard liquors, light drinking habits were already impossible for many people. However, bootlegged whiskey was not the same as pre-Prohibition whiskey. In the New York City Medical Examiner's Office, confiscated bottles were often tested. Some bootlegged whiskeys were 60 percent alcohol; some were even 100 percent alcohol. They also discovered that most of the alcohol being sold around the city was industrial alcohol.

The government had placed regulations on industrial alcohol since 1909 that required it to be made poisoned, or denatured, to deter people from drinking it. Organized crime organizations had chemists on their payroll to chemically alter the stolen industrial alcohol to remove the poison. Wood alcohol, a common industrial alcohol, was a serious concern: 1 teaspoon (5 mL) could cause blindness, and 1 cup (250 mL) could kill a person in just a few hours. Additionally, the process of renaturing or redistilling industrial alcohol often did not work. When it did not work, there would be an outbreak of alcohol deaths in an area. Drinkers were risking not only their health, but also their lives.

The Treasury Department said that 60 million gallons (227,124,707 L) of industrial alcohol were stolen every year by the mid-1920s. This was often the work of organized crime groups stealing large amounts at once, not individual people stealing 1 gallon (3.8 L). A judge in Manhattan summed it up best while giving remarks in court in 1920: "Prohibition is a joke. It has deprived the poor workingman of his beer and it has flooded the country with rat poison."[36]

Many of these concoctions were diluted with water and flavored with various ingredients in an attempt to make them taste like whiskey or another liquor. Fancy, ornate labels were pasted on the bottles to deceive their customers into thinking they were buying genuine products. All too often, the filtering methods failed or were not used at all. As such, the processed beverages sickened, paralyzed, and killed thousands of Americans.

Prohibition in New York City

In 1926, Representative Fiorello La Guardia, who later became mayor of New York City, called 20 newspaper reporters and photographers to his office in the House of

Survival Favors the Wealthy

Breaking the law during Prohibition was not uncommon for wealthy Americans. They could even afford the luxury of frequent "booze cruises," a legal way to drink alcohol by taking advantage of international waters along the U.S. coasts. Journalist Deborah Blum also pointed out that money ensured safe drinking, noting that "the wealthy lovers of jazz-flavored cocktails … could afford the pricey higher-quality alcohol on the market. Many of them routinely invited their bootleggers to parties, gaining some personal insurance against poisoning."[1]

Prohibition produced a very different set of circumstances for the poor. The price they paid to drink was often very steep. In 1926 alone, more than 400 people died in the poor neighborhoods of New York City, greatly exceeding alcohol-related deaths in those areas before Prohibition. One of the worst culprits was "smoke," a cloudy-looking cocktail made by mixing water and fuel alcohol. Even though it killed people, it was popular among the poor because it cost little money. Regarding smoke, Blum wrote, "government agents trying to hunt down suppliers of the poor man's cocktail swore that it was served right from cans stenciled with the word POISON—and that people didn't care. They just gambled that it wouldn't kill them and drank it anyway."[2]

Across the South and Southwest, Jamaican Ginger, or Jake, had been a popular cocktail for many years because it was cheap to produce. Now the cocktail was being made with denatured alcohol. As many as 15,000 drinkers were stricken with a paralyzing effect that was called Jake-foot after the cheap cocktail that caused it. Jake-foot caused people to have limp muscles in their feet, which would dangle loosely from their leg. To walk, they had to lift their leg up high and the foot would flop down with the toes hitting the pavement first.

1. Deborah Blum, *The Poisoner's Handbook: Murder and the Birth of Forensic Medicine in Jazz Age New York.* New York, NY: Penguin Books, 2010, pp. 157–158.

2. Blum, *The Poisoner's Handbook*, p. 52.

Representatives' House Office Building in Washington, D.C. Once the crowd gathered, he took "near beer" (the low-alcohol beer allowed under the Volstead Act) and mixed it with a bottle of malt tonic that was legally purchased at a pharmacy. He declared the alcoholic beverage legal and drank it as the media representatives took pictures.

La Guardia intended for his stunt to mock Prohibition laws. Police at the scene were so confused about whether the lawmaker had broken a law that they did nothing. Newspapers across the country carried the story. Soon, groceries everywhere stocked their shelves with malt tonic, and Americans flocked to buy it.

Prohibition was so greatly ignored in New York City that there were said to be 30,000 speakeasies in operation throughout the city. Lerner used this story about the visit of a German mayor to New York City to show how ineffective Prohibition was there:

> *When the Mayor of Berlin, Gustav Boess, visited New York City in the fall of 1929, one of the questions he had for his host, Mayor James J. Walker, was when Prohibition was to go into effect. The problem was that Prohibition has already been the law of the United States for nearly a decade. That Boess had to ask tells you plenty about how well it was working.*[37]

Not that ignoring Prohibition was an easy solution for New Yorkers. Before Prohibition, there were around a dozen alcohol poisoning patients per year at Bellevue Hospital in the Kip's Bay neighborhood of Manhattan, three of whom died. However, during Prohibition, those numbers drastically increased:

Fiorello La Guardia had his secretary, M. M. Fisher, taste the beer he made in his congressional office in 1926. He also made the beer for other members of the House of Representatives.

The Speakeasy Life

In many cities, the number of speakeasies easily outnumbered the number of saloons in pre-Prohibition days. In Rochester, New York, the number of speakeasies was actually double the number of saloons the city once housed, and that ratio was common for most other large cities. New York City had an estimated 30,000 speakeasies, many in parts of the city, such as business districts and middle-class neighborhoods, which had previously not permitted saloons.

To enter, a person had to know not only the location of the speakeasy but also the secret code word that served as added security against Prohibition agents, which lent a sense of excitement and allure. A speakeasy visitor described the experience:

Every time you go for a drink there is adventure. I suppose it adds to one's pleasure to change into a pirate or a dark character entering a smuggler's cave. You go to locked and chained doors. Eyes are considering you through peepholes in the wooden walls ... You sign your name in a book and receive a mysterious-looking card with only a number on it. And you are admitted to a back-parlour bar with a long row of loquacious (talkative) drinkers. There may be a red signal light which can be operated from the door in case of a revenue [Prohibition] officer or police demanding entrance.[1]

1. Quoted in Deborah Blum, *The Poisoner's Handbook: Murder and the Birth of Forensic Medicine in Jazz Age New York*. New York, NY: Penguin Books, 2010, p. 51.

The sheer volume of speakeasies operating in many large cities was representative of the loose enforcement of the law.

In 1926 the hospital had treated 716 people for alcoholic hallucinations, blindness, and even paralysis due to poisoned alcohol. Sixty-one of those patients had died. And that figure didn't include deaths due to chronic alcoholism—those had numbered 87 in 1918 ... [In 1927] more than 700 city residents would drink themselves to death by year's end.[38]

When 23 people died and 89 were hospitalized at Bellevue after Christmas 1926 celebrations, Charles Norris—Chief Medical Examiner for the City of New York—issued a public attack on Prohibition: "The government knows it is not stopping drinking ... [and] must be charged with the moral responsibility for the deaths that poisoned liquor causes."[39]

The Rise of Pharmacies

Although bootlegged alcohol received the most of the liquor profits during Prohibition, pharmacists also profited due to sales of legal "medicinal whiskey," a hard liquor that was 95 percent alcohol. Before Prohibition, pharmaceutical hard liquor was just one remedy on a list of many remedies.

However, during Prohibition, doctors suddenly prescribed alcohol for everything. From anxiety to a toothache and from the flu to pain management, alcohol was suddenly a cure for almost anything. Legions of doctors wrote prescriptions for themselves and friends to obtain "medicines" that contained whiskey—something permitted by the Volstead Act. Some physicians even took bribes to write phony prescriptions for their patients.

Prescriptions for medicinal whiskey increased 400 percent during Prohibition. In fact, Walgreens became a pharmacy chain today thanks to the "drug store boom" during the Prohibition era. Illegal liquor sellers capitalized on the opportunity pharmacies presented, opening speakeasies that pretended to be drug stores as a front for their illegal trade. Pharmacists were also part of another scam, obtaining large amounts of medicinal alcohol from government warehouses that they would then sell to bootleggers.

Smuggling by Land and Sea

The spirit of lawlessness in the 1920s turned many people into criminals. Smugglers drove trucks loaded with bottles and kegs of liquor in from Mexico and Canada. Sailing ships, nicknamed "rumrunners," hauled secret cargoes of liquor from the Bahamas, Cuba, and Europe to points of entry from New York to Florida. Smugglers were also busy along the Pacific coastline from Washington to California.

Smugglers themselves occasionally became victims of other criminals on the high seas. Pirates often roamed

The U.S. Coast Guard was responsible for patrolling the country's water borders to seize boats called rumrunners that were attempting to illegally transport liquor into the country.

the coasts, spying on the activities of smugglers. They would overtake rumrunners and hold up the crews at gunpoint, demanding the cash the smugglers had just received for their deliveries.

An Era of Organized Crime

Crime organizations existed long before Prohibition, but it was the illegal liquor market that truly established them as profitable, which increased both their success and the level of danger. Gangsters now had control over a source of revenue that had once been divided over an entire industry of breweries and distilleries. Since these massive profits were not taxed and were being shared among substantially fewer people than the industry of alcohol production had once supported, it should come as no surprise that organized crime evolved during Prohibition. The system of criminals and the political allegiances needed to continue their work grew exponentially because money bought power.

In some places, organized crime operated through armed thugs who used intimidation and violence to extort payments from bootleggers, moonshiners, smugglers, and owners of speakeasies. Elsewhere, they set up their own liquor-making operations. With millions of dollars in revenue at stake, rival gangs in America's big cities eventually collided. They fought, often violently, over control of the liquor trade in various regions, especially when a crime syndicate tried to open operations in the territory of another. Gangsters bribed, threatened, beat, and killed anyone who got in their way, including police, Prohibition agents, and elected officials.

Law enforcement officials during the 1920s classified the gangs into two groups. Those in the rural areas and small towns of the West, Midwest, and South were known as outlaws. They were generally native-born Americans who committed robbery, kidnapping, and murder. City gangsters, meanwhile, were called mobsters. These criminals were often immigrants or the children of immigrants who took part in criminal organizations known as syndicates. Some urban neighborhoods teemed with Irish, Jewish, and other gangs, but the most powerful and notorious were Italian mobsters, such as those of the Mafia.

The Reign of Al Capone

The most notorious Italian mobster was Al Capone, a ruthless killer whose rise during Prohibition came to symbolize the collapse of law and order in Chicago, Illinois. After avoiding legal prosecution for killing two men in Brooklyn, New York, Capone moved to Chicago, and by the late 1920s, he ran Chicago's most powerful crime syndicate. He was responsible for operating a network of businesses that brought in $60 million a year through an army of about 1,000 mobsters:

Jack "Legs" Diamond was an Irish-American gangster who operated out of New York during Prohibition. A few days after he was found not guilty of kidnapping and torture, he was shot and killed.

As a former petty thug and book-keeper, Capone brought both his street smarts and his expertise with numbers to [mobster Johnny] Torrio's Chicago operations. Torrio recognized Capone's skills and quickly promoted him to partner ...

In 1923, when Chicago elected a reformist mayor who announced that he planned to rid the city of corruption, Torio and Capone moved their base beyond the city limits to suburban Cicero. But a 1924 mayoral election in Cicero threatened their operations. To ensure they could continue doing business, Torrio and Capone initiated an intimidation effort on the day of the election, March 31, 1924, to guarantee their candidate would get elected. Some voters were even shot and killed.[40]

In addition, Capone was able to avoid prosecution for murder for years by paying off both public officials and police and threatening witnesses.

The St. Valentine's Day Massacre

Capone skillfully avoided arrests, political pressure, and revenge from his enemies in his armor-plated Cadillac. Although authorities could never prove his guilt, Capone was believed to have arranged the brutal murders of numerous rival gangsters. One of the killings he was suspected of having organized shocked the nation in its brutality.

On Valentine's Day in 1929, seven men stood in a cold city garage, waiting for a liquor delivery. They were in Bugs Moran's gang, a rival of Capone's gang. Suddenly, a car drove up. Out stepped four men, two dressed as police. Moran's men, possibly thinking this was a routine police raid, dropped their guns and lined up before a wall with their hands above their heads. The two other men accompanying the uniformed men took out submachine guns and opened fire, hitting the captives with more than 150 bullets. The mobsters who were dressed as police pretended to arrest the gunmen and sped away in the car. It was all a murderous hoax.

Although gangland murders would take the lives of around 500 mobsters in Chicago during Prohibition, the St. Valentine's Day Massacre struck a public nerve with its boldness. Suspicion fell immediately upon Capone, but he was in Florida at the time of the slayings. He eventually did go to prison, but not for the vicious crimes he committed. Instead, federal prosecutors convicted him of tax evasion.

Chicago was hardly the only major American city infested with gangland violence. Gangs flourished in other big cities, such as New York; Kansas City, Missouri; Miami, Florida; and Philadelphia, Pennsylvania. Americans became both fascinated and horrified with newspaper reports of gangsters and

Born in Brooklyn, Capone spent his youth as a petty criminal in a rough neighborhood. A knife gash to his face left him known for the rest of his life as Scarface.

Shown here is a crowd gathering after a gang massacre in Kansas City, Missouri, in the 1930s.

their criminal activities.

Law Enforcement Problems

From its very beginning, Prohibition was not allocated the proper resources to be enforced adequately. At the federal level, only 1,520 agents were hired in 1920, although that would double within a decade. Still, it was never enough people to control the nation's borders, let alone its cities.

Making matters worse, corruption was rampant. Numerous Prohibition agents, along with many policemen, members of the Coast Guard, judges, and political officials turned a blind eye

to wrongdoings after taking bribes from criminals. Fiorello La Guardia once joked that New York City alone would require a police force of 250,000 men and another force of 250,000 to "police the police."[41] An average of one of every twelve federal agents was fired annually for accepting bribes.

Because of the high number of arrests during Prohibition—even though most lawbreakers were never apprehended— American courtrooms faced a backlog of cases that led to many shortcuts in the legal process. Overworked judges set up "bargain" days that allowed defendants to skip a trial, plead guilty, and avoid

A group of federal agents can be seen in this photograph with boxes of alcohol recovered from a raided speakeasy.

a stiff sentence. Juries often showed contempt for Prohibition by acquitting defendants who were probably guilty of trafficking alcohol.

Izzy and Moe

Honest law enforcement officials, however, did exist. Two Prohibition agents, Isidor "Izzy" Einstein and Moe Smith, made more than 4,932 arrests by themselves, 95 percent of which ended in conviction. In fact, they made 20 percent of all Prohibition arrests in New York. Together, they seized 5 million bottles of alcohol and busted 100 speakeasies a week.

Using wigs, false moustaches, and false noses, Izzy and Moe showed up at speakeasies as concert musicians, Ivy League college students, members of European royalty dressed in tuxedoes, and elderly ladies. Izzy even once impersonated a Chinese launderer and another time a Russian fisherman, as well as:

> *football players (when arresting an ice cream vendor who sold out of his cart), Texas rangers, a Yiddish couple (Smith playing the wife), streetcar conductors, gravediggers, fishermen, and ice men. Einstein—who had a booming baritone—once introduced himself as an opera*

Izzy and Moe are shown here wearing regular clothes in the top photograph and wearing disguises in the bottom photograph.

singer and gave a rousing performance in a speakeasy before closing it down.[42]

By 1925, Izzy and Moe were known worldwide. However, it was likely their fame that led to their being fired that year. Izzy and Moe's supervisors became embarrassed over their antics. "The service must be dignified," a government spokesman suggested, while explaining the dismissal of the two men. "Izzy and Moe belong on the vaudeville stage [a form of popular entertainment]."[43]

Enforcement Budget Balloons

The federal government appropriated $6.5 million for the first year of enforcement of Prohibition, but it proved to be far too little. A few years later, Prohibition Bureau officials requested almost five times that amount.

States that passed Prohibition enforcement laws also generally did not adequately fund the necessary number of police officers, judges, clerks, bailiffs, prison wardens, prison guards, and others. In response to growing expenses, many state officials backed away from enforcing Prohibition. Some argued that because Congress took the lead in pushing for Prohibition, the federal government should assume most of the responsibility for enforcement.

As state and federal officials bickered, the number of Prohibition violations continued to rise.

The Government's Chemists

By the 1920s, government chemists had devised almost 70 formulas to denature industrial alcohol, many involving adding more wood alcohol. Bootleggers' inventive chemists had to work hard to crack the government's formulas and renature these new industrial alcohol formulas. Since the government chemists' formulas were quickly cracked by the bootleggers' chemists, the government knew it needed a new strategy. In 1926, government chemists went on the offensive, "developing a secret project in the aid of Prohibition."[44] Warnings were also issued: "Drinking was about to become more risky."[45]

On December 31, 1926, the Treasury Department announced that all formulas must now contain at least double the amount of wood alcohol added to industrial alcohol during denaturing, bringing the content to nearly 10 percent wood alcohol. Outcries were met with a curt defense: the decision was "simple law enforcement."[46]

The new denaturing protocol also involved poisons such as kerosene, gasoline, brucine, iodine, zinc, mercury, nicotine, ether, formaldehyde, chloroform, camphor, carbolic acid, and acetone. However, it was the massive increase in wood alcohol that led to the most deaths. In 1927, anti-prohibition congressmen tried to pass a law blocking the Treasury Department's deadly decision, but they were defeated during voting. The response from prohibitionist congressmen was telling:

In 1926, government chemists released nearly a dozen new formulas to counter bootlegging successes in renaturing, but each new formula was quickly cracked by the better-paid bootleg chemists.

"No one would be dead if people simply obeyed the law and tried to live in a morally upright fashion."[47]

Criticism of the Government Chemists

The outcry against the government's deliberate poisoning of alcohol was fierce. The New York City Medical Examiner's office railed against "the government's deliberate poisoning of alcohol … [and] having their national government adopt a policy now to kill people in droves."[48] Famous actor, cowboy, and writer Will Rogers famously said, "governments used to murder by the bullet only. Now it's by the quart."[49]

Eventually, the government responded to the criticism of their industrial alcohol denaturing process. In 1931, government chemists released a new formula that used leftover petroleum products from gasoline processing. It smelled awful, but it was non-toxic. The Treasury Department, desperate to change public opinion about Prohibition, hosted a press event for the new formula, inviting journalists to Washington, D.C., to taste the new formula. However, the public did not care about the smell, the new formula, or anything else the Treasury Department had to say. People cared about the death toll. Blum wrote, "The idea was to scare people into giving up illicit drinking. Instead, by the time Prohibition ended in 1933, the federal poisoning program, by some estimates, had killed at least 10,000 people."[50]

President Hoover's Wickersham Commission

Secretary of Commerce Herbert Hoover was elected president in 1928. He was a public supporter of Prohibition, although he did not practice abstinence during Prohibition, as he "regularly stopped by the Belgian embassy on his way home from Commerce. Since the embassy was technically on foreign soil, he could drink there legally and be guaranteed some very good-quality alcohol as well."[51]

His presidential predecessors, Warren G. Harding and Calvin Coolidge, had done little to address the negative consequences of Prohibition. Hoover kept a campaign promise to appoint a high-level national commission staffed by respected educators, lawyers, and judges to investigate Prohibition. Headed by George W. Wickersham, a highly respected barrister, the commission spent 19 months and $500,000 analyzing the impact of the 18th Amendment. The commission conducted public hearings to collect testimonies and data from a wide range of supporters and critics of Prohibition. Hopes ran high across the country that the Wickersham Commission would help Americans understand if national liquor abolishment was working.

In some ways, the Wickersham Commission had an accurate sense of Prohibition's failings. The commission revealed that alarming numbers of Prohibition agents were fired each year for corruption or unwillingness to perform their duties. The commission also admitted that it was not possible to have a national law succeed when some states did not support it and other states supported it but did not want to enforce it. The commission stated,

The Wickersham Commission, led by George W. Wickersham, shown here, acknowledged the numerous challenges of enforcing the 18th Amendment, but a majority of the commission's members still opposed repealing the amendment.

much of the difficulty comes from the rigidity of the Eighteenth Amendment and of the National Prohibition Act, which prescribe one unbending rule for every part of the country and every type of community without regard to differences of situation or conditions or to public opinion.[52]

The Wickersham Commission understood that some people who had supported the 18th Amendment from the temperance movement were now major contributors to public opinion against Prohibition because of the harshness of the law. Further, it doubted that Prohibition would have even passed had it not been for World War I, when a large part of the adult drinking population was away in active military service and patriotism moved many Americans to give up personal rights for the greater good of the nation. These were all astute observations of social climate and public opinion.

In other ways, however, the commission was tone deaf, and the logic of bootleggers, smugglers, gangsters, and others who defied Prohibition was beyond their comprehension. Regarding the excess of successful smuggling into international border cities, Wickersham wrote, "All that is required is a little more intelligence, a little more patriotism, a little more cooperation, and a little more will to succeed."[53]

The Wickersham Commission concluded that the disorganization and corruption of Prohibition enforcement affected how local governments viewed and enforced it, pointing to four amendment sessions, two reorganizations of the federal leadership system, and three rewrites of the permit system for industrial alcohol in the first eleven years. The disorganization, Wickersham concluded, was due to the government assuming incorrectly that the law held power because it was federal, and therefore would work without need for enforcement. The government, Wickersham wrote, clearly did not understand the magnitude of such a task or have any idea how to handle or organize a federal police force. "It was an experiment, the extent and difficulty of which was probably not appreciated [by the government],"[54] Wickersham wrote.

The Wickersham Commission's suggestions for improving the enforcement of Prohibition included editing the 18th Amendment or the Volstead Act or both in an effort to organize the laws enforcing Prohibition into a plan, though it also admitted,

Those who say that prohibition has not been effective probably expect too much from the law agencies of enforcement … It is a confession that prohibition can not prohibit; that the object of prohibition is to prevent the use of intoxicating liquors, because that use is harmful; and here is a confession that the object can not be accomplished. The answer is that no more ought to be expected of enforcement of prohibition than of other statutes making it unlawful to do certain acts. Courts cannot deal effectively with acts that can be done in private.[55]

When the commission published its findings, it managed to disappoint both sides of the controversy because it took no side. Prohibitionists and anti-prohibitionists both condemned the committee's work. Nevertheless, the word "repeal" gained popularity. More and more Americans confessed to strong misgivings about Prohibition and wanted the law repealed or at least modified to make wine and beer legal.

Chapter Six

THE PUSH FOR REPEAL

The case against Prohibition grew stronger with each passing day. As Lerner wrote, "it [was] very clear that in many parts of the United States more people were drinking, and people were drinking more."[56]

Americans held a wide variety of opinions about why Prohibition should be repealed. The national ban on alcohol was supposed to reduce crime and corruption, improve social problems, lessen the number of prisons, and improve health and hygiene. When the Volstead Act first went into effect, liquor consumption went down by 30 to 50 percent. Arrests for drunkenness also fell. However, these gains proved to be temporary. Additionally, many felt the rise in the use of drugs such as opium and cocaine was directly attributed to the lack of access to safe alcohol options.

The defiance of Prohibition bred contempt for the law. The crime wave led by gangsters terrified the public, as did the climbing alcohol poisoning death toll. States such as Maryland and New York made virtually no effort to participate in enforcement, undermining the law and its chance to succeed. It simply did not work.

The Press Supports Repeal

Many urban newspapers that had once played a big role in supporting the crusade to ban alcohol now featured editorials in favor of doing away with, or weakening, Prohibition. Small-town newspapers, which were more likely to support Prohibition, were disappearing as their readers relocated to the nation's cities in search of new jobs. Prohibitionists railed against these papers as propaganda, but the momentum was growing.

The *Chicago Tribune* printed a strong opinion:

Normally, no American govern-ment would engage in such busi-ness. It would not and does not set a trap gun loaded with nails to catch a counterfeiter. It would not put "Rough on Rats" on a cheese sand-wich even to catch a mail robber. It would not poison postage stamps to get a citizen known to be misusing the mails. It is only in the curious fanaticism of Prohibition that any means, however barbarous, are considered justified.[57]

Organized Resistance to Prohibition

Long before the Wickersham Com-mission issued its report, the national protest movement against Prohibition was underway. It was led by a new organization, the Association Against the Prohibition Amendment (AAPA). The first national anti-Prohibition organization was founded before Pro-hibition even went into effect in 1918 by William H. Stayton, a former naval officer and lawyer. Stayton recruited professionals, university leaders, judg-es, military leaders, elected officials, and businessmen opposed to Prohibi-tion on the grounds that government did not have the authority to criminal-ize personal liberty. These respected and influential individuals were hard to dismiss.

Due in part to the work of the AAPA, the tide of public opinion began to change. Adopting some of the same methods used by the ASL, the AAPA raised large sums of money to sup-port anti-prohibition candidates, kept track of voting records in Congress, and funded articles and research that favored their cause. Unlike the ASL, however, the AAPA employed the tal-ents of advertising professionals to run a public relations campaign.

One of its tactics was to point out the connection between Prohibition and crime. Another was to satirize prohi-bitionists as Puritans opposed to life's pleasures. Drinking alcohol, they said, was normal and respectable. The AAPA also wanted to be seen by the public as being reasonable. The letterhead on the organization's stationery stated, "Beer and Light Wines NOW; But No Saloons EVER."[58]

The AAPA had powerful allies in industries. Business tycoon Pierre S. du Pont spoke for many wealthy busi-nessmen when he pointed out that "the income tax would not be necessary in the future and half the revenue required for the [federal government's] budget … would be furnished by the tax on liquor alone."[59] Other business leaders, however, simply thought that Prohibi-tion had not lived up to expectations. John D. Rockefeller, an oil-refining titan and a teetotaler, had once given finan-cial support to the ASL, but now said, "it is my profound conviction that the benefits of the Eighteenth Amendment are more than outweighed by the evils that have developed and flourished since its adoption."[60]

Prohibition-Probes

★ **We do not want the old time saloon, but was it any worse than the speakeasy, bootlegger, blackmailer, gangster and hypocrite?**

ASSOCIATION AGAINST THE PROHIBITION AMENDMENT

The Association Against the Prohibition Amendment (AAPA) managed an effective public relations campaign by pointing out that Prohibition had created new societal problems that rivaled or even dwarfed those the movement had intended to solve.

More Organizations for Repeal

Founded in May 1929 by Pauline H. Sabin, the wife of a well-known New York banker, the Women's Organization for National Prohibition Reform (WONPR) attracted more than 1 million members within 2 years. The WONPR's mission statement read:

We are convinced that National Prohibition, wrong in principle, has been equally disastrous in consequences in the hypocrisy, the corruption, the tragic loss of life and the appalling increase of crime which have attended the abortive attempt to enforce it.[61]

The American Bar Association—the professional organization for attorneys— also came out against Prohibition and was joined by the American Federation of Labor, the nation's largest labor union.

A Shift in Values

The rise of popular support for repeal

revealed that values had changed dramatically in American society. Many of the nation's older, more deeply rooted values and beliefs of thrift, hard work, and godliness had been nurtured by centuries of traditional, Christian life in rural and small-town America. In contrast to these were the values born of a new, modern, and technology-based way of life. The late social scientist John C. Burnham believed there was clear evidence to show that "ideas of dominant groups of Americans about what was acceptable and respectable began to turn upside down as the campaign to undermine Prohibition gathered momentum."[62] This inversion of values was common among young people, especially in urban areas.

World War I also led young people to reconsider traditional ideas of right and wrong. Many members of this generation experienced a disillusionment born from seeing the dark side of human nature. Millions of young Americans led their lives with a new pessimism that the next man-made tragedy would happen soon enough. Breaking taboos, which included drinking illicit liquor, became normal for millions of postwar young Americans.

A powerful new medium—the motion picture—was used to push the repeal agenda. By the end of the decade, an estimated 110 million Americans went to movie theaters every week. Many of these films depicted heroes drinking bootleg alcohol in a positive light. Comedies, meanwhile, often ridiculed supporters of Prohibition as being hopelessly pious and narrow-minded. Motion pictures also glamorized romance, which may have helped to undermine traditional beliefs.

Finally, revolutionary ideas about human psychology, evolution, communism, time, and space challenged traditional biblical teachings, thus weakening the authority many ministers had over drinking and drinkers.

The Great Depression

Many Americans were angered that Prohibition had diverted millions of dollars from the economy into the hands of criminal thugs and corrupt federal agents. Most of the 1920s had been a prosperous time for America. However, in October 1929, the stock market crashed, bringing about the Great Depression. Thousands of businesses and banks collapsed, and millions of Americans lost their savings and their jobs. The United States, along with nations around the world, sunk into a catastrophic economic depression. The nation's capitalistic economic system—once considered the mightiest in the world—had failed, with no signs of immediate recovery.

Millions of Americans now looked to the federal government for help. Legions of unemployed people looked to those missing tax revenue dollars as money that should have been available to aid their suffering. Ridding the nation of Prohibition would put millions of people back to work in distilleries, breweries, transportation, and retail. The alcohol restrictions had, many believed, contributed to the economy's collapse because it closed profitable industries, eliminating thousands of jobs. Prohibition was seen as a forced annihilation of liquor making, distributing, and selling businesses, jobs, and industries. "Money had a lot to do with the change in the nation's attitude toward prohibition—money rather than morals,"[63] the late historian Donald Barr Chidsey observed.

As for government financial concerns, tax revenues from alcohol sales were too precious to ignore in the desperate times of the 1930s. The government was doubly in trouble because of the unintended costs of enforcing Prohibition. Lerner explained,

> *Before Prohibition, many states relied heavily on excise taxes in liquor sales to fund their budgets. In New York, almost 75% of the state's revenue was derived from liquor taxes ... At the national level, Prohibition cost the federal government a total of $11 billion in lost tax revenue, while costing over $300 million to enforce.*[64]

The 18th Amendment was not intended to be a costly endeavor; prohibitionists assumed people would willingly follow the new laws. The budget for the Bureau of Prohibition began at $4.4 million with around 1,000 agents on staff. The government quickly saw that this was not enough, and within a few years, there would be four times as many agents and $13.4 million per year budgeted to the Prohibition Bureau and $13 million per year budgeted to the Coast Guard. Thornton wrote, "to those amounts should be added the expenditures of state and local governments"[65] on Prohibition enforcement.

After in-depth analysis, Thornton concluded that "the only beneficiaries of Prohibition were bootleggers, crime bosses, and the forces of big government."[66]

Tough Times for Teetotalers

Loyal enemies of alcohol were convinced that their social movement was now deeply entrenched in American society. A campaign to repeal a constitutional amendment seemed to many to be impossible. At least, it had never been done before. Senator Morris Sheppard of Texas observed in September 1930 that "there is as much chance of repealing the Eighteenth Amendment as there is for a hummingbird to fly to the planet Mars with the Washington Monument tied to its tail."[67]

Prohibition's apologists, however, were losing energy, revenue, legitimacy, and public support. For one thing, ever since accomplishing their goal, the nation's major dry Prohibition organizations, such as the ASL, had difficulty keeping their members excited and supportive of Prohibition. Membership and contributions declined after the

Volstead Act went into effect. When the Great Depression arrived, financial support dropped even more. Gone, too, was the intense crusading spirit and the sense of purpose that once united millions of Americans.

Worse yet, the ASL's effective, brilliant leader, Wayne B. Wheeler, died in 1927.

Wheeler's successor was James Cannon Jr., a bishop in the Methodist Episcopal Church in the South. A stern, conservative man, Cannon had a strong puritanical streak that went well beyond Prohibition. He railed not only against drinking alcohol, but also against playing cards, soft drinks, and taking walks on Sundays. He lacked, however, the leadership skills to motivate millions of prohibitionists. The league was incapable of competing with the better organized, well-funded, and committed AAPA.

National polls indicated a growing public support for repeal that alarmed prohibitionists. In 1930, *Literary Digest* conducted a national survey that revealed that majorities in all but five states favored repealing Prohibition. A poll taken by the Newspaper Enterprise Association in 47 states showed that almost half of the respondents wanted Prohibition to be weakened while 31.3 percent wanted full repeal. Teetotalers were a minority once again, it seemed.

The Momentum of Repeal

Sensing the new national sentiment, many politicians also changed course. During the 1932 presidential election, many Republicans favored giving the states the option of deciding for themselves whether to legalize liquor. The Democratic Party firmly backed its candidate, Franklin D. Roosevelt, on his desire to repeal Prohibition. His campaign theme "Happy days are here again" was embraced with wide enthusiasm, and he won 42 of the 48 states in the general election.

On February 20, 1933, Congress voted to repeal the 18th Amendment and decided that a new amendment must be written. The House and Senate quickly wrote and approved the 21st Amendment, but it could not become law until it was ratified by three-fourths of the 48 states, or 36 states.

Although the amendment was given seven years for the ratification process before expiration, the federal government wanted to move things along more quickly than that. The states were given an ultimatum, requiring them to call special conventions for the ratification vote. In the meantime, the federal government also began loosening some of the rules of Prohibition, such as permitting the sale of beer again.

Repeal would not need seven years to be ratified. The movement had an incredible momentum. In April, Michigan and Wisconsin became the first two states to approve the 21st Amendment. By the end of the summer,

Eleanor Roosevelt's Take on Repeal

First Lady Eleanor Roosevelt's father, brother, and uncles were alcoholics, and this greatly influenced her life. Her parents died before she turned 10. She was sent to school in England because her grandmother could not protect her from her uncles, who drank heavily. As a result of her childhood experiences, she had a strong opinion about liquor, yet it was her husband who repealed the Prohibition law.

Eleanor Roosevelt had a news column that ran in papers across the country for nearly three decades. On July 14, 1939, she explained her position on the issues of Prohibition and its repeal:

> Little by little it dawned upon me that this law was not making people drink any less, but it was making hypocrites and law breakers of a great number of people. It seemed to me best to go back to the old situation in which, if a man or woman drank to excess, they were injuring themselves and their immediate family and friends and the act was a violation against their own sense of morality and no violation against the law of the land.
>
> I could never quite bring myself to work for repeal, but I could not oppose it, for intellectually I had to agree that it was the honest thing to do. My contacts are wide and I see a great many different groups of people, and I cannot say that I find that the change in the law has made any great change in conditions among young or old in the country today.[1]

1. Quoted in "Eleanor Roosevelt's Take on the Day," PBS, accessed January 22, 2018. www.pbs.org/wgbh/americanexperience/features/eleanor-my-day/.

25 states had ratified the amendment. Once repeal was in motion, many Americans left Prohibition behind altogether. Businesses began applying for liquor licenses. Many hotel bars reopened. The federal government had given permission for almost 125 million gallons (473,176,473 L) of liquor to be produced in anticipation of the law passing. The U.S. Brewers Association said that in July 1933, Americans drank more than 1 billion glasses of beer. By November, City Hall in Manhattan was receiving 1,000 requests for liquor licenses a day, and 33 states had ratified the amendment.

The 21st Amendment

The only way to undo an amendment is another amendment. Therefore, to end Prohibition, the 21st Amendment was necessary. The amendment stated,

Section 1.

The eighteenth article of amendment to the Constitution of the United States is hereby repealed.

Section 2.

The transportation or importation into any state, territory, or possession of the United States for delivery or use therein of intoxicating liquors, in violation of the laws thereof, is hereby prohibited.

Section 3.

This article shall be inoperative unless it shall have been ratified as an amendment to the Constitution by conventions in the several states, as provided in the Constitution, within seven years from the date of the submission hereof to the states by the Congress.[1]

1. "21st Amendment," Cornell Law School, accessed January 22, 2018. www.law.cornell.edu/constitution/amendmentxxi.

Three states—Ohio, Pennsylvania, and Utah—had votes scheduled for December 5, 1933. Ohio and Pennsylvania voted to ratify the amendment early in the day. Utah, the last state needed to complete ratification, did so at exactly 5:32 p.m. Eastern Standard Time.

National prohibition was dead.

That evening, newly elected President Roosevelt issued a proclamation declaring that alcoholic beverages were again legal. He added,

I ask the wholehearted cooperation of all our citizens to the end that this return of individual freedom shall not be accompanied by the

repugnant conditions that obtained prior to the adoption of the 18th Amendment and those that have existed since its adoption. Failure to do this honestly and courageously will be a living reproach to us all.

I ask especially that no State shall by law or otherwise authorize the return of the saloon either in its old form or in some modern guise.[68]

Celebrations Across the Nation

On December 5, 1933, Prohibition came to an end, with President Franklin D. Roosevelt declaring, "what America needs now is a drink."[69] It was too late for many businesses to celebrate the occasion, but those who planned ahead were ready to celebrate as soon as Utah's vote came across the wire:

The well-prepared hotels rolled out bar carts, wheeling them through the lobbies to dispense cocktails. Bloomingdale's department store had been savvy enough to acquire its own liquor permit, and the moment the radio flashed news of the Utah vote, it sold waiting customers bottles of imported scotch and rye. The line at Bloomingdale's snaked out the door and into the noisy, shouting, jubilant streets.[70]

Epilogue

THE EFFECTS OF PROHIBITION

The liquor trade was once again legal in the United States, but the country still felt the lingering effects of Prohibition in the decades that followed. The most significant and long-lasting effect of Prohibition was the regulation of other sources of addiction, such as gambling and drugs. The legal precedence for dealing with addiction that exists today has a strong moral component linked back to the days of Prohibition.

The nearly 14-year-long "noble experiment" left the country forever changed. Thankfully, repeal reversed some of the more devastating issues of Prohibition, such as organized crime, corruption, and job availability. Alcoholism was also put on a path of healthier recovery after repeal, as organizations such as Alcoholics Anonymous began offering support services and scientists began research into addiction, cirrhosis, and other drinking-related illnesses.

Effects Still Seen in State Laws Today

The 21st Amendment did not totally repeal all bans on drinking. Prohibition, in fact, remained in some counties and states for decades, thanks to section two of the amendment. The wording of this passage was intended to allow those states wishing to remain dry to reject shipments of alcohol from wet states.

Although Prohibition is now more than seven decades gone, many states still enforce Prohibition-era restrictions on the purchase of alcohol. Pennsylvania, for example, only allows the sale of wine and liquor in 600 special state-run stores. Wal-Mart has been in a legal battle with the state of Texas since 2015 because of a state law that

After Prohibition was repealed, President Franklin D. Roosevelt's daughter, Anna (third from left), hosted a German beer festival to celebrate the 21st Amendment.

prevents public companies with more than 35 shareholders from selling hard liquor.

Massachusetts, Pennsylvania, Idaho, and other states even have quotas for the number of liquor licenses that can be issued to bars and restaurants, which has led to black market sales of liquor licenses. There are reports of sales of liquor licenses in Montana for $1 million and New Jersey for $1.6 million. Idaho, one of the most extreme examples of liquor licensing restrictions, only allows 1 license per every 1,500 people.

There are also still hundreds of dry counties across the United States today that lose tax income every day to neighboring wet counties.

blue laws still on the books	blue law repeals	
Alabama	Connecticut	2012
Indiana	Georgia	2011*
Minnesota	Arkansas	2009*
Mississippi	Washington	2009**
Montana	Colorado	2008
North Carolina	New York	2008
Oklahoma	Virginia	2008***
South Carolina	Kentucky	2004
Tennessee	Rhode Island	2004
Texas	Ohio	2004
Utah	Idaho	2004
West Virginia	Kansas	2004
*makes it a local option	Delaware	2003
**only a specific number of stores are	Pennsylvania	2003
allowed to stay open on Sundays	Massachusetts	2003
***only in cities with 100,000+ people	Oregon	2002

Prohibition-era "blue laws," or laws that ban the sale of liquor on Sundays, still exist in 12 states. This chart shows those states, as well as states that repealed their blue laws and the years those laws were repealed. There are also hundreds of counties across the United States that restrict alcohol sales partially or completely.

Aftermath of Prohibition

Despite the passage of the 21st Amendment, a widespread fear of Prohibition's return haunted many Americans for decades after repeal took effect. Knowing well how changing economic and moral concerns could shut down businesses and industries, many in the liquor industry remained vigilant for signs of any renewed interest in Prohibition. They were quick to launch propaganda attacks against writers and professors who spoke out against alcohol. Local governments that dared to let citizens vote on new temperance laws could also count on facing the wrath of the liquor interests.

Prohibitionists were angry about the repeal for many years. Some bitter supporters of Prohibition remained convinced that powerful businessmen immorally used their wealth and influence to lead the nation away from Prohibition merely for their own economic benefit.

Policy-Making Changed Forever

The repeal of America's noble experiment plays a role in modern debates about most social ills. Many Americans wonder: If the federal government can no longer restrain adult consumption of alcohol, why does it then have the right to try to curb other social problems, such sex working, gambling, and the use of illicit drugs such as marijuana and cocaine? One thing is clear: Those who consider these issues must first study the rich and complex history of temperance, prohibition, and repeal in the United States.

Thornton wrote that the lessons of Prohibition should be applied not only to the war on drugs, but also to tobacco and cigarette legislation, insider trading, abortion, gambling, and censorship of all forms. However, the most important lesson of Prohibition is, as Lerner wrote, "the Constitution is no place for experiments, noble or otherwise."[71]

Notes

Introduction: Americans and Alcohol

1. Ed Crews, "Rattle-Skull, Stonewall, Bogus, Blackstrap, Bombo, Mimbo, Whistle Belly, Syllabub, Sling, Toddy, and Flip: Drinking in Colonial America," *Colonial Williamsburg*, Spring 2007 issue. history.org/foundation/journal/holiday07/drink.cfm.

2. Eric Burns, *The Spirits of America: A Social History of Alcohol*. Philadelphia, PA: Temple University Press, 2004, p. 17.

3. Burns, *The Spirits of America*, p. 18.

4. Quoted in Edward Behr, *Prohibition: Thirteen Years That Changed America*. New York, NY: Arcade, 1996, p. 14.

5. "Stars, Stripes and … a Secret Sauce? Founding Fathers and Their Drinking Habits," flaviar.com, July 4, 2015. flaviar.com/blog/stars-stripes-anda-secret-sauce.

6. W. J. Rorabaugh, *The Alcoholic Republic: An American Tradition*. New York, NY: Oxford University Press, 1979, p. 151.

7. Richard H. Thornton, *An American Glossary: Being an Attempt to Illustrate Certain Americanisms Upon Historical Principles: Vol. I. A–L*. Philadelphia, PA: J. B. Uppincott Company, 1912, p. 98.

8. Quoted in Alice Felt Tyler, *Freedom's Ferment*. Minneapolis, MN: University of Minnesota Press, 1944, p. 310.

Chapter One: Early Attempts at Prohibition

9. Quoted in Burns, *The Spirits of America*, p. 47.

10. Quoted in Daniel J. Boorstin, *The Americans: The Colonial Experience*. New York, NY: Random House, 1958, p. 82.

11. Quoted in Steve Simon, "Alexander Hamilton and the Whiskey Tax," Alcohol and Tobacco Tax and Trade Bureau, U.S. Department of the Treasury, last updated September 4, 2012. www.ttb.gov/public_info/special_feature.shtml.

12. Quoted in Behr, *Prohibition*, p. 17.

Chapter Two: The Movement Toward Prohibition Begins

13. Quoted in Rorabaugh, *The Alcoholic Republic*, p. 43.

14. Quoted in J. C. Furnas, *The Americans: A Social History of the United States 1587–1914*. New York, NY: Putnam, 1969, p. 503.

15. Lyman Beecher, "The Nature and

Occasions of Intemperance," University of Virginia, accessed January 16, 2018. utc.iath.virginia.edu/sentimnt/sneslbat.html.

16. Quoted in Behr, *Prohibition*, p. 24.
17. Quoted in Behr, *Prohibition*, p. 22.
18. Quoted in Furnas, *The Americans*, p. 512.
19. Quoted in James Gray, *Why Our Drug Laws Have Failed and What We Can Do About It: A Judicial Indictment of the War on Drugs*. Philadelphia, PA: Temple University Press, 2001, p. 122.
20. Burns, *The Spirits of America*, p. 94.

Chapter Three:
The Rebirth of the
Prohibition Movement

21. Carol Mattingly, *Well-Tempered Women: Nineteenth-Century Temperance Rhetoric*. Carbondale, IL: Southern Illinois University, 2001, p. 42.
22. Donald Barr Chidsey, *On and Off the Wagon: A Sober Analysis of the Temperance Movement from the Pilgrims Through Prohibition*. New York, NY: Cowles, 1969, p. 2.
23. Quoted in William T. Ellis, *"Billy" Sunday: The Man and His Message: With His Own Words Which Have Won Thousands for Christ*. Philadelphia, PA: John C. Winston Company, 1917, p. 101.
24. Carry Amelia Nation, *The Use and Need of the Life of Carry A. Nation*. Topeka, KS: F. M. Steves & Sons, 1908, p. 130.

25. Quoted in "Carrie Nation," PBS. www.pbs.org/wgbh/amex/1900/peopleevents/pande4.html.
26. Quoted in "A Saloon Wrecked," *Phillipsburg Herald*, January 3, 1901. www.newspapers.com/newspage/79822785/.
27. Quoted in Fran Grace, *Carry A. Nation: Retelling the Life*. Bloomington, IN: Indiana University Press, 2001, p. 176.

Chapter Four:
The 18th Amendment

28. Quoted in Richard Mendelson, *From Demon to Darling: A Legal History of Wine in America*. Berkeley, CA: University of California Press, 2009, p. 61.
29. Mark Thornton, "Cato Institute Policy Analysis No. 157: Alcohol Prohibition Was a Failure," Cato Institute, July 17, 1991. object.cato.org/pubs/pas/pa157.pdf.
30. Michael Lerner, "Unintended Consequences," PBS, accessed January 22, 2018. www.pbs.org/kenburns/prohibition/unintended-consequences/.
31. Thornton, "Cato Institute Policy Analysis No. 157."
32. Deborah Blum, *The Poisoner's Handbook: Murder and the Birth of Forensic Medicine in Jazz Age New York*. New York, NY: Penguin Books, 2010, p. 49.

Chapter Five:
Lawlessness Ravages
the Country

33. Lerner, "Unintended Consequences."
34. Burns, *The Spirits of America*, p. 194.
35. Thornton, "Cato Institute Policy Analysis No. 157."
36. Quoted in Blum, *The Poisoner's Handbook*, p. 51.
37. Lerner, "Unintended Consequences."
38. Blum, *The Poisoner's Handbook*, p. 158.
39. Blum, *The Poisoner's Handbook*, pp. 154–155.
40. "Al Capone," History.com, accessed January 22, 2018. www.history.com/topics/al-capone.
41. Quoted in Robert Maddox, "The War Against Demon Rum," in *American History Volume 2: Reconstruction Through the Present*, ed. Robert Maddox. Guilford, CT: Dushkin, 1989, p. 102.
42. Blum, *The Poisoner's Handbook*, p. 65.
43. Quoted in Burns, *The Spirits of America*, p. 245.
44. Blum, *The Poisoner's Handbook*, p. 152.
45. Blum, *The Poisoner's Handbook*, p. 152.
46. Blum, *The Poisoner's Handbook*, p. 153.
47. Blum, *The Poisoner's Handbook*, p. 163.
48. Blum, *The Poisoner's Handbook*, pp. 157–158.
49. Thornton, "Cato Institute Policy Analysis No. 157."
50. Deborah Blum, "The Chemist's War," *Slate*, February 19, 2010. www.slate.com/articles/health_and_science/medical_examiner/2010/02/the_chemists_war.html.
51. Blum, *The Poisoner's Handbook*, pp. 156–157.
52. George W. Wickersham, "U.S. National Commission on Law Observance and Enforcement: Publications No. 1." Washington, DC: U.S. Government Printers Office, 1929, p. 81.
53. Wickersham, "U.S. National Commission on Law Observance and Enforcement," pp. 26–27.
54. Wickersham, "U.S. National Commission on Law Observance and Enforcement," p. 20.
55. Wickersham, "U.S. National Commission on Law Observance and Enforcement," p. 14.

Chapter Six:
The Push for Repeal

56. Lerner, "Unintended Consequences."
57. Blum, *The Poisoner's Handbook*, pp. 159–160.
58. Quoted in John C. Burnham, *Bad Habits: Drinking, Smoking, Taking Drugs, Gambling, Sexual Misbehavior and Swearing in American History*. New York, NY: New York University Press, 1994, p. 433.
59. Quoted in Burnham, *Bad Habits*, p. 46.
60. Quoted in Jean Edward Smith, *FDR*.

New York, NY: Random House, 2007, p. 267.

61. "Excerpt from WONPR Convention, April 23–24, 1939," Women's Organization for National Prohibition Reform, accessed January 23, 2018. www.wonpr.org/history.htm.

62. Burnham, *Bad Habits*, p. 24.

63. Chidsey, *On and Off the Wagon*, p. 128.

64. Lerner, "Unintended Consequences."

65. Thornton, "Cato Institute Policy Analysis No. 157."

66: Thornton, "Cato Institute Policy Analysis No. 157."

67. Quoted in Chidsey, *On and Off the Wagon*, p. 127.

68. Franklin D. Roosevelt, "187–Proclamation 2065–Repeal of the 18th Amendment," American Presidency Project, accessed January 23, 2018. www.presidency.ucsb.edu/ws/index.php?pid=14570.

69. Jennifer Latson, "A Toast to the End of Prohibition," *TIME*, December 5, 2014. time.com/3605609/a-toast-to-the-end-of-prohibition/.

70. Blum, *The Poisoner's Handbook*, p. 241.

Epilogue:
The Effects of Prohibition

71. Lerner, "Unintended Consequences."

For More Information

Books

Bearce, Stephanie. *Gangsters and Bootleggers: Secrets, Strange Tales, and Hidden Facts About the Roaring 20s*. Waco, TX: Prufrock Press, 2016.
Bearce's book details the Prohibition era, including organized crime and criminals such as Al Capone.

Binder, John J. *Al Capone's Beer Wars: A Complete History of Organized Crime in Chicago During Prohibition*. Amherst, NY: Prometheus Books, 2017.
This book covers the history of organized crime in Chicago during the Prohibition era.

Davis, Marni. *Jews and Booze: Becoming American in the Age of Prohibition*. New York, NY: New York University Press, 2012.
Once Prohibition arrived, Jewish people in America were forced to choose between abandoning their history and culture and remaining outside the American mainstream, and this book details that struggle.

Engdahl, Sylvia. *Amendments XVIII and XXI: Prohibition and Repeal*. Farmington Hills, MI: Greenhaven Press, 2009.
This book includes an analysis of the impact of both amendments relating to Prohibition, and it discusses modern parallels.

Websites

Nucky's Empire: The Prohibition Years
www.acmuseum.org/nucky-s-empire-the-prohibition-years.html
This website from the Atlantic City, New Jersey, Public Library features an online exhibition about Prohibition in Atlantic City.

Prohibition: **A Film by Ken Burns and Lynn Novick**
www.pbs.org/kenburns/prohibition
This three-part documentary film series details the rise and fall of Prohibition, and the website includes photographs and essays.

Temperance & Prohibition
www.prohibition.osu.edu
This website is an excellent online source for Prohibition information from the history department at the Ohio State University, featuring essays, images, and primary source material.

The Temperance Exhibit
lostmuseum.cuny.edu/archive/exhibit/temperance
This website features primary sources from the temperance movement in an online museum exhibition format.

Index

A
Alcoholics Anonymous, 89
alcoholism, 65, 89
alcohol poisoning, 62, 80
American Bar Association, 82
American Civil War, 31
American Federation of Labor, 82
American Revolution, 9, 12, 17–18
American Temperance Society, 6
    22–23
Anti-Saloon League (ASL), 45,
    47–49, 52, 81, 84–85
arrests, 21, 43, 45, 69, 71–72, 80
Association Against the Prohibition
    Amendment (AAPA), 81–82, 85

B
Baraboo, Wisconsin, 34
bargain days, 72
bathtub gin, 57
Beecher, Lyman, 22, 24–25, 29
Bellevue Hospital, 62, 65
Blum, Deborah, 61, 76
Boess, Gustav, 62
bootlegged alcohol, 58, 60, 65, 74, 83
booze cruises, 61
Boston, Massachusetts, 6, 9, 22, 26
breweries, 67, 84
Burnham, John C., 83
Burns, Eric, 9, 31, 57

C
California, 33, 65
Cannon, James, Jr., 85

Capone, Al, 67, 69–70
chemists, 60, 74–76
Chicago, Illinois, 7, 38, 67, 69
Chicago Tribune, 80
Chidsey, Donald Barr, 38, 84
civil liberties, 52
Clark, Billy James, 21
Coast Guard, 66, 71, 84
Cold Water Army, 26–28
Colonial Williamsburg Foundation, 8
Columbus, Christopher, 8
Coolidge, Calvin, 76
crime, 31, 60, 67, 69, 80–82, 85, 89

D
Declaration of Independence, 12–13,
    18
Democratic Party, 85
denaturing, 60–61, 74, 76
"Directions for Preserving the Health
    of Soldiers," 20
distilleries, 15, 17–18, 22, 57, 67, 84
Dow, Neal, 29–31
drug stores, 65

E
Edwards, Justin, 26
Einstein, Isidor "Izzy," 72–74
enforcement, 29, 52, 54, 56, 64, 71,
    74, 78–80, 84

F
Florida, 65, 69, 71

G

gangsters, 7, 67–69, 71, 78, 80
Georgia, 14–17, 22, 45, 54
Great Depression, 83, 85
Greeley, Horace, 14

H

Hamilton, Alexander, 18
Harding, Warren G., 76
Hoover, Herbert, 76
"hot waters," 8

I

Idaho, 90
immigrants, 31, 67
Independent Order of Good
    Templars, 27
industrial alcohol, 60, 74, 76, 78
*Inquiry into the Effect of Spirituous
    Liquors on the Human Body and
    Mind, and Their Influence upon the
    Happiness of Society, An* (Rush), 6,
    19

J

Jake, 61
Johnson, William "Pussyfoot," 43–45

K

Kansas, 41, 43, 45
Kenyon, William S., 47
Kilman, Marvin, 12
Kramer, John F., 54, 56

L

La Guardia, Fiorello, 60, 62–63, 71
Lerner, Michael, 53, 57, 62, 80, 84, 92
Lewis, Diocletian, 33
Lincoln, Abraham, 31

liquor licenses, 29, 86, 90
Literary Digest, 85
London Trustees Act, 15
Lusitania, 47

M

Maine, 29–31, 45
Martha Washington Societies, 26
Maryland, 26, 80
Matthews, Mark, 26
McKinley, William, 43
Medical Examiner's Office, New
    York City, 56, 60, 65, 76
medicinal whiskey, 65
Mellen, W. R. G., 25
Michigan, 31, 85
Mississippi, 45, 51
mobsters, 67, 69
molasses, 9, 15
Montana, 90
moral thermometer, 19–20
Moran, Bugs, 69
motion pictures, 83
"Mother Thompson and her Visita-
    tion Band," 33

N

Nation, Carry, 41–43
near beer, 61
Nebraska, 7, 31, 43, 52
New Jersey, 90
Newspaper Enterprise Association,
    85
New York City, 40, 56, 60–62, 64, 71,
    76
noble experiment, 89, 91
North Carolina, 45, 47
North Dakota, 45

O

Oglethorpe, James, 15–16, 22, 54
Ohio, 33–34, 36, 45, 54, 86–87
Oklahoma, 44–45
outlaws, 67

P

Pennsylvania, 17–18, 31, 49, 71, 86–87, 89–90
pharmacists, 65
pirates, 67
poisons, 74
Prohibition Bureau, 54, 74, 84
Puritans, 8, 15, 81

Q

Quakers, 17, 29

R

renaturing alcohol, 60, 74–75
repeal, 31, 77, 79–80, 82–87, 89–92
Rochester, New York, 64
Roosevelt, Eleanor, 86
Roosevelt, Franklin D., 85, 87–88, 90
Roosevelt, Theodore, 45
Rorabaugh, W. J., 12
rum, 6, 8–9, 12, 15, 18, 20, 28, 31, 36, 53
rumrunner, 65–67
Rush, Benjamin, 6, 18–22

S

Sabin, Paulie H., 82
17th Amendment, 47
Sheppard, Morris, 84
Six Sermons on the Nature, Occasions, Signs, Evils and Remedy of Intemperance (Beecher), 22
16th Amendment, 47

Smith, Moe, 72–74
smoke, 61
smugglers, 15, 64–65, 67, 78
Sons of Temperance, 27
speakeasies, 62, 64–65, 67, 72, 74
Stayton, William H., 81
St. Valentine's Day Massacre, 7, 69
Sunday, Billy, 38–41, 54

T

Taft, William Howard, 47
tax revenue, 83–84
teetotaler, 22, 81, 84–85
Templars of Honor and Temperance, 27
Tennessee, 45
Texas, 72, 84, 89
Thompson, Eliza J., 33
Thornton, Mark, 53, 60, 84, 92
Topeka Daily Capital, 43
Treasury Department, 60, 74, 76
triangular trade, 6, 9
21st Amendment, 7, 85, 87, 89–91

U

Union Temperance Society of Moreau and Northumberland, 21
U.S. Brewers Association, 86
U.S. Congress, 7, 18, 31, 36, 47–50, 52–53, 74, 81, 85, 87
U.S. Department of Agriculture, 57
U.S. House of Representatives, 50, 61
U.S. Senate, 6–7, 47, 49–50, 85
Utah, 87–88

V

Volstead Act, 7, 52–53, 59, 61, 65, 78, 80, 85

Volstead, Andrew J., 52

W

Walgreens, 65

Wal-Mart, 89

War-Time Prohibition Act, 51

Washington, D.C., 36, 38, 45, 49, 61, 76

Washington, George, 12, 18

Washingtonian Temperance Society, 26–27

waterborne disease, 8

Webb, Edwin Y., 47

Wheeler, Wayne B., 45–46, 49, 52, 85

Whiskey Rebellion, 6, 18

Wickersham Commission, 76–78, 81

Wickersham, George W., 76–78

Willard, Frances, 36, 38

Wilson, Woodrow, 48, 52

Wisconsin, 34, 85

Woman's Christian Temperance Union (WCTU), 6, 36–38, 41, 43, 49

women's crusades, 33–35

Women's Organization for National Prohibition Reform (WONPR), 82

wood alcohol, 60, 74

World War I, 47, 51, 54, 78, 83

Picture Credits

Cover, p. 6 (bottom) Buyenlarge/Getty Images; pp. 4–5, 7 (top right), 62–63, 71, 72 Bettmann/Bettmann/Getty Images; p. 6 (top) Topical Press Agency/Getty Images; pp. 7 (top left, bottom left), 24, 35, 39, 40–41, 44, 46, 58, 75, 77 Courtesy of the Library of Congress; p. 7 (bottom right) Chicago History Museum/Getty Images; pp. 10–11 North Wind Picture Archives; p. 12 Private Collection/Photo © Don Troiani/Bridgeman Images; p. 13 Parhamr/Wikimedia Commons; pp. 16–17 The Print Collector/Print Collector/Getty Images; p. 19 Wellcome Collection; p. 23 Archives & Special Collections at Amherst College; p. 27 Yale University Art Gallery; p. 28 Fotosearch/Getty Images; p. 30 Library of Congress/Corbis/VCG via Getty Images; p. 37 David J. & Janice L. Frent/Corbis via Getty Images; pp. 42 (main), 66, 68 Historica Graphica Collection/Heritage Images/Getty Images; p. 42 (inset) The New York Historical Society/Getty Images; p. 55 De Agostini Picture Library/A. Dagli Orti/Bridgeman Images; p. 64 Hulton Archive/Getty Images; p. 70 Courtesy of the National Archives Catalog; p. 73 Underwood and Underwood/The LIFE Picture Collection/Getty Images; p. 82 Prohibition Probe postcard. Association Against the Prohibition Amendment postcards and stationery (Accession 2005.204). Hagley ID: 2005204_038. Courtesy of the Hagley Museum and Library; p. 90 ullstein bild/ullstein bild via Getty Images.

About the Author

With masters and undergraduate degrees in Art History, **Joan Stoltman** brings a unique perspective when she writes about general history. She studies it by seeing first what experiences were recorded by artists, designers, craftspeople, and architects. Her favorite part of writing nonfiction is the research and learning. Joan is a regular at her local library in Buffalo, New York, and is always trying to find an interesting biography or new nonfiction release (or 10) that she can devour. Her reading partner is her Chihuahua, Cliffy. Her life partner is her husband, Todd. Both play their role in making her life possible.